Love, Remember

Love, Remember

40 Poems of Loss, Lament and Hope

Malcolm Guite

CANTERBURY
PRESS
Norwich

© Malcolm Guite 2017

First published in 2017 by the Canterbury Press Norwich
Editorial office
3rd Floor, Invicta House
108–114 Golden Lane
London EC1Y 0TG, UK
www.canterburypress.co.uk

Canterbury Press is an imprint of Hymns Ancient & Modern Ltd
(a registered charity)

H
Y Ancient
M
N &Modern
S

Hymns Ancient & Modern® is a registered trademark of
Hymns Ancient & Modern Ltd
13A Hellesdon Park Road, Norwich,
Norfolk NR6 5DR, UK

Bible quotations are from the New Revised Standard Version of the
Bible, Anglicized Edition, copyright © 1989, 1995 by the Division of
Christian Education of the National Council of the Churches of Christ
in the USA. Used by permission. All rights reserved.

British Library Cataloguing in Publication data

A catalogue record for this book is available
from the British Library

978 1 78622 001 1

Typeset by Regent Typesetting
Printed and bound in Great Britain by
CPI Group (UK) Ltd

Contents

vii

wk 4

Introduction

This book is written to give voice both to love and to lamentation, to find expression for grief without losing hope, to help us honour the dead with tears, yet still to glimpse through those tears the light of resurrection. It is written in the conviction that the grief that we so often hide in embarrassment, the tears of which some people would want to make us ashamed, are the very things that make us most truly human. Grief and lament spring from the deepest parts of our soul because, however bitter the herbs and fruits they seem to bear, their real root is Love, and I believe that it is Love who made the world and made us who we are.

Why should we need to make the case for giving place and even permission to our lamentation, our grief and our tears? Surely, such grief is the most natural thing in the world and should be met always with compassion, perhaps even a kind of admiration for the courage bereaved people show in expressing grief, actively summoning the painful memories of those they have loved and lost. Yet we live in a culture that averts the eyes from death and is embarrassed at every reminder of mortality. We live in a culture of the 'quick fix', the easy answer, the so-called 'power of positive thinking'. Once we had a positive tradition of mourning, a time set aside for it, with all its own customs and rituals, sympathies and consolations. We used to have a culture that gave us a time to weep as well as a time to celebrate: now, we are rushed straight to the celebration and even that is no consolation, for we all have to pretend that there is nothing to be consoled about.

So funerals, which should mark and lament loss, name and confront death, are rebranded as 'celebrations of life'. This insist-

ence on giving everything an instant and positive spin has begun
to fill me with unease. This unease was crystallised for me in a
brief and now nearly ubiquitous quotation from Canon Henry
Scott Holland, which is often presented as a poem usually titled
'Death is Nothing at All':

Death is nothing at all. It does not count. I have only slipped
away into the next room. Nothing has happened. Everything
remains exactly as it was. I am I, and you are you, and the old
life that we lived so fondly together is untouched, unchanged.
Whatever we were to each other, that we are still. Call me by
the old familiar name. Speak of me in the easy way which you
always used. Put no difference into your tone. Wear no forced
air of solemnity or sorrow. Laugh as we always laughed at the
little jokes that we enjoyed together. Play, smile, think of me,
pray for me. Let my name be ever the household word that it
always was. Let it be spoken without an effort, without the
ghost of a shadow upon it. Life means all that it ever meant.
It is the same as it ever was. There is absolute and unbroken
continuity. What is this death but a negligible accident? Why
should I be out of mind because I am out of sight? I am but
waiting for you, for an interval, somewhere very near, just
round the corner. All is well. Nothing is hurt; nothing is lost.
One brief moment and all will be as it was before. How we
shall laugh at the trouble of parting when we meet again!

Now I must tread delicately, as this oft-quoted passage may, quite
understandably, be a favourite with some readers of this book,
and I do not doubt that it has brought comfort, real comfort, to
thousands, for there is, or rather *there can be*, real truth in it. I
too live in the Christian hope that we, and those we have loved
and lost, will together see the *final* truth of these words of conso-
lation. One day we will know that 'life means all it ever meant';
we will look back from the glory of resurrection on death as a
'negligible accident' and rejoice to know that 'all is well'. But
that is not where we are when this passage is handed to us on
a shiny card by the funeral director, or when it is read at the

funeral. Taken on their own, so soon after the shock of bereavement, these 'comforting' words about death can paradoxically seem like a deadly lie: a 'quick fix' appearance of happiness that only makes the grieving feel guilty for their grief.

For taken by themselves, at that point in our grieving, these words are simply not true: something terrible *has* happened, a seemingly irrevocable disaster, something inexplicable, blind and ruthless. We have been cut off from our belovèd in mid-conversation; the line has gone dead with so much left to do and say. There is a gap, a breach, a shadow, and we are left stunned and sickened by its severity. If death is nothing at all, why did it have to happen? If death is nothing at all, why did the Son of God himself go through it with such sorrow, pain and cries of dereliction? Indeed, this little passage, as it is usually quoted and used at funerals, seems to me so empty of the depth and resonance of the Bible, with Christ in his dying and rising so absent from it, that I could scarcely credit that it was written by a Christian, let alone by a canon of St Paul's Cathedral! I decided to find the original context and read for myself the sermon from which it was taken.

What a revelation that proved to be! This passage has been cut clean away, lifted out of a sermon that deals more profoundly, honestly and courageously with the reality of death than almost anything I have ever read. It is as though with this passage someone has swiftly copied out the answer to a question without knowing what the question was, or 'cribbed' the answer to a difficult sum without being able to show any of the 'working out'. The original sermon was preached in St Paul's on 15 May 1910 after the death of Edward VII, and Holland addresses not only the death of a monarch, but the reality of death as we all encounter it. Right from the beginning of the sermon he gives full, clear and courageous expression to the shock and reality of grief. Here is what he says about death in the very opening of the sermon:

It is the supreme and irrevocable disaster. It is the impossible, the incredible thing. Nothing leads up to it, nothing prepares for it. It simply traverses every line on which life runs, cutting across every hope on which life feeds, and every intention which gives life significance. It makes all we do here meaningless and empty.

And he laments, as we all must if we are honest, how cruel and random it seems when death strikes.

But how often it smites, without discrimination, as if it had no law! It makes its horrible breach in our gladness with careless and inhuman disregard of us.

Then he goes on to show that shock and lamentation in the face of death are deeply embedded in scripture: our cry is the cry of the Word and the cry of all the world:

So the Scripture cried out long ago. So we cry in our angry protest, in our bitter anguish, as the ancient trouble reasserts its ancient tyranny over us today. It is man's natural recoil. And the Word of God recognizes this and gives it vigorous expression.

So how does Scott Holland move from these cries of pain to the serene and more familiar passage, beginning 'Death is nothing at all' and ending, as it is often quoted, with the comforting words:

All is well. Nothing is hurt; nothing is lost. One brief moment and all will be as it was before. How we shall laugh at the trouble of parting when we meet again!

At first he gives voice to both of them, to what he calls 'two ways of regarding death, which appear to be in hopeless contradiction with each other'. All honour to him that he does give voice to *both* of them, that he speaks for those who feel the grief as well as for those who feel and know the consolation. But he does more than that; he sets himself, and us, a real task:

Our task is to deny neither judgement, but to combine both. The contrasted experiences are equally real, equally valid. How can they be reconciled? That is the question.

The scriptural text of his sermon is 1 John 3.2-3:

> Beloved, now are we the sons of God, and it doth not yet appear
> what we shall be: but we know that, when he shall appear we
> shall be like him, for we shall see him as he is.

As he opens out this text Scott Holland seeks the reconciliation
of these two contrasting responses to death, where all reconcili-
ation is to be found: in the life, death and resurrection of Jesus.
Yes, death is a terrible thing, but it is a terrible thing that God
faces for us and we face it with him and in him, in Christ. Our
life is 'hid with Christ in God; we face death with the promises
and the assurance of God. We are already his beloved children
and it doth not yet appear what we shall be.'

As Scott Holland says later in the sermon, 'Already we are in
Jesus; already we are of his body and yet it doth not yet appear
what we shall be.' And in the sermon he dwells compassionately
on the 'not yet', for we are living in an 'in between' time, in one
way still shadowed by death, in another lit by the promise of
morning and resurrection.

As I read through this remarkable sermon, so much began to
make sense. The famous passage that seems a facile denial when
read torn out of context gains much greater authority, trust-
worthiness and comfort when set against these other passages
of the sermon which give such compassionate voice to our grief
and fear. These 'contrasted experiences' are indeed 'equally real,
equally valid' and can both be given expression fully and brought
to Christ.

So if we are agreed that it is a mistake to rush to the easy answer
or the 'quick fix', and that the words of Henry Scott Holland
are weakened rather than strengthened by being separated from
their context in a sermon that expresses pain as well as joy,
how might we best restore the fullness, the range of experience
and expression for all of us who have loved and lost? I hope
that *Love, Remember* will offer some help in restoring that full
range of expression, in making the poetry of loving lamentation
available in a new way. Love cannot help but remember; remem-

brance cannot help but weep. We yearn for trust, recovery and hope and hardly know whether, when or how to trust that hope, but perhaps the poetry in this book can help us as we feel our way forward.

In recent times, a secular model has suggested five stages of grief. The Kübler-Ross model, first posited in 1969, tracks a progressive journey from *denial* through *anger, bargaining* and *depression*, towards *acceptance*. This is all very well, but as any grieving person will tell you, nobody makes this journey smoothly, evenly and in that order, though some well-meaning people can sometimes make us feel guilty for not doing so. These five stages all represent real experience, but they are often going on at the same time, switching back and forth between one another, contradicting and obscuring one another. There will be poetry in this anthology that in some way expresses the reality of all these stages. Another limitation of this model is that it is closed, secularised and in a strange way almost medicalised. It has no place for sudden grace, inexplicable glimpses of hope, intimations of immortality. It uses words like anger and depression but seems to have little space for the rich mix of remembrance, love and lament that sometimes brings not only peace but wisdom to the bereaved.

And yet, however roundabout it may have to be, there *is* a journey, there are staging posts, there is a movement from the first shock of loss to a place where grace can be known and hope can be rekindled. We never move backwards to being the same person again as we were before our loss. Even our once-familiar joys and comforts – the country walk, the familiar book, the conversation of friends – are experienced differently, when we are able to take them up again. And though we may often feel that we are making it utterly alone, it is a journey that many have made before us: brave souls, wise souls, and happily for us, some of them great poets. They have done a little mapping for us, left notes behind for us to find, so that we too can give voice to what we are going through. In these pages I want to gather those scraps of the map and those scattered leaves. I want to recover and renew the words of love, lamentation and hope that have been uttered for us and before us and put those words into your hands so that when you need them you might also have them in your hearts.

Turning back to those consolation cards and quotations so kindly provided by funeral directors and sent by well-meaning friends, it seemed to me that while there is a place for them, there is a need for something more. I decided to look back into the great treasury of English poetry, so much of it written before our hasty age, before our modern aversions to and inhibitions about death, and search for poems that might give voice to grief and hope, to shadow and light.

So who is this book for? First, it is for the bereaved, and here again I must tread delicately. I have known some grief myself, but not the extremities that I have witnessed in my life as a priest. I know that words can only go so far. Some of the mightiest poets seeking to express their grief have made it clear how little even their best words can do. We shall be accompanied at various points in this journey together by verses from Alfred, Lord Tennyson's searingly honest grief journal *In Memoriam*. Even he says:

> I sometimes hold it half a sin
> To put in words the grief I feel;
> For words, like Nature, half reveal
> And half conceal the Soul within.
> (Section V)

But he also sees that it is still worth trying for he goes on to say:

> But, for the unquiet heart and brain,
> A use in measured language lies;
> The sad mechanic exercise,
> Like dull narcotics, numbing pain.
> (Section V)

Indeed, much later on in the work, explaining that it is not really one monolithic poem but a series of brief lyrics, a scattering of questions whose answers can never be more than partial and provisional, he says:

> If these brief lays, of Sorrow born,
> Were taken to be such as closed
> Grave doubts and answers here proposed,
> Then these were such as men might scorn:
> (Section XLVIII)

What Tennyson offers, instead are

> Short swallow-flights of song, that dip
> Their wings in tears, and skim away
> (Section XLVIII)

To the bereaved, who alone will know the depths of their own sorrows, I would say the same: take all the poems in this book as 'short swallow-flights of song' and if they 'dip their wings' in your tears then perhaps that will provide some relief, even as they skim away.

This book is also for the friends of the bereaved: cautious, afraid, hesitant, sometimes feeling strangely cut off, hardly knowing whether it is best to visit or not to visit (it is always best to visit!); wondering, when they do visit, what to say and what not to say, always feeling that they can't possibly know what is really going on in their friend's heart. The chance to overhear, in these pages, the frank confessions, the cries of both pain and joy of poets who have gone before us, might offer some clues about keeping and deepening friendship with those who grieve.

Lastly, this book is for all of us, trapped in a glib and shallow age, caught up in this conspiracy of evasion, this complicity in denial, this costly aversion from the eyes of death. Perhaps some of these poems will help us to take off the blinds, turn off the distractions, and face death with clarity and courage.

The plan of this book

Although I have reservations about the 'stages of grief', I have nevertheless felt that this book would be best patterned as a journey. This begins before a death itself occurs, upon the 'Brinks and Edges' of death, and so that is the title of the book's first part. From that brink we fall or are hurled into the 'Shock of Loss' (Part 2), the sheer numbness, confusion and fear of grief. As C. S. Lewis observed in the opening sentences of his classic book *A Grief Observed*, 'No one ever told me that grief felt so like fear.'

Though the sense of shock and loss may return many times, and at other phases and stages of our journey, beyond that shock there is what I have called 'Loving Lament'. To have loved at all is to have opened yourself to the possibility of lament. That openness and vulnerability is part of what we offer to someone by loving them in the first place. In that sense, lamentation is itself, however painful, a kind of loving, a keeping of a promise. Then, somewhere in the midst of lamentation, we begin to encounter memory in a new way. The 'Remembrance of Things Past' becomes both a delight and a despair. Such remembrance is *tender* in the full sense of that word; tender in its loving but also tender to the touch, like an open wound, and yet the memory that opens the wound is also searching it, cleansing it and healing it. 'Love, remember' is perhaps the most poignant and tender thing that Ophelia says in that strange brink and interlude between the death of her father and the death to which she goes. But when that tender remembrance of things past, which is a kind of holding on, has begun its healing work then there can also be, paradoxically, a letting go, and the fifth part of this book draws together some of the poetry of that letting go. It is not a letting go of love, or a letting go of memory or even of grief, rather it is letting a life go free, letting the belovèd go deep into God from whom we come and to whom we will return.

We need to let go in order to receive. In spite of the first shock and emptiness, the sense of unjust deprivation, our long experience of grief can eventually open us up to receiving real gifts: wisdom, empathy and compassion, which might have been received in no other way. Of course, this is not something we can or should say to ourselves or anyone in the first shock of grief. Perhaps we can never say it to another person, but we can come to know for ourselves that in and through our grieving we have received gifts given in no other way.

Finally, there is 'Hope' (Part 7). There is the great hope given and centred in the death and resurrection of Jesus Christ. That central act and turning point of the cosmos radiates in all directions through time and space. It is mirrored and imaged in every sunrise, given expression in every spring; even our daily awakening and uprising speak of it. But we cannot truly know it for what it is until it comes to us, unlooked for, late in our journey. So these are not the stages themselves but perhaps the seven staging posts on our journey.

Who are the poets who will accompany us? I have drawn from all the ages; Shakespeare is there in all his classic familiarity, but he stands cheek by jowl with young poets whose work has only just been published. The great names are there: Shelley lamenting Adonais and John Donne telling death not to be so proud. But there are poets less well known who have given voice to things we need to say. The classic canon of English literature is for historical reasons filled mainly with the names of men, but in grief we (and especially *we men*) need to hear the voice of women – Christina Rossetti and Elizabeth Barrett Browning from the nineteenth century, Luci Shaw and Carol Ann Duffy from our own time – giving us unique insights. Some poets leave us just a single leaf to gather on this journey, while some are more constant companions. I have summoned Tennyson in particular to walk with us and meet us at each of our staging posts. I have already drawn in this Introduction on his poem *In Memoriam*, written over the course of more than a decade after the death of his belovèd friend Arthur Hallam in 1833. It is the grief journal, the prayer diary, the jottings along the road of the first three years of Tennyson's bereavement. It is so honest and compelling, yet so little read these days, that I felt it would be good to use passages from it that will assist us on our journey, acting as a kind of prelude to each of our 'staging posts'.

How to use this book

This is an anthology into which one might simply dip, searching
through the parts for a particular poem or finding the words that
express or match a mood as it is needed. It might be used as a
resource to find language for yourself, for a friend, or for a service
or memorial: words that give expression to what needs to be said
on that specific occasion. But one could also use this book as a
companion for the journey of grief itself, or as a means to accom-
pany a friend who is making that journey. Most religions in their
earlier traditions have set aside a special period, somewhere
between 30 and 40 days, for a first intense and companioned
encounter with mourning. In Judaism this was called Shiat: first,
seven days of private grief, then a further 30 of accompanied
lamentation. In the Catholic Church there was a tradition of 40
days of mourning, matching and balancing the 40 days of Lent.
This book is organised so that this journey can be taken with the
poets over 40 days. For each day there is the offered nourishment
of a poem and my prose reflection on it. However you use this
book, I hope that it will give expression to loving remembrance,
and that you will find, as Tennyson did, that 'it is better to have
loved and lost than never to have loved at all'.

PART I

Brinks and Edges

*Before and beyond the threshold
of death*

Introduction

Death is a threshold, not simply for those who cross from this life into the presence of the living God, those who tread the verge of Jordan, those who will be welcomed as Christian was in *A Pilgrim's Progress*.

> When the day that he must go hence was come, many accompanied him to the river-side, into which as he went, he said, 'Death, where is thy sting?' And as he went down deeper, he said, 'Grave, where is thy victory?'
>
> So he passed over, and all the trumpets sounded for him on the other side.

Death is not just a threshold for the dying, it is a threshold for the living and the grieving too. Like a river heard far off, we come to its brink, knowing it will be there: knowing that there will be a descent and a crossing, and that the landscape on the farther side will be different. In this part of the book I have chosen poems about coming to that brink, poems of anticipation, about crossing into grief itself, and about the first look back to the dreadfulness of the event.

To open up the poetry of brinks and edges I would like to reflect particularly on the passage in Hamlet from which the title of this book is taken. In a most poignant scene, a grief-stricken Ophelia gives a sprig of rosemary to Queen Gertrude, saying: 'There's rosemary, that's for remembrance; pray you, love, remember.' These words might be addressed to all of us.

In many ways Hamlet is the play par excellence about death and grieving, about the breach and rift that death makes in the fabric of our lives and the sense all mourners have of standing on a perilous edge. The play opens with the rift opened in Denmark by the death of Hamlet's father. Young Hamlet's friend, Horatio, seeing the extremity of his grief, fears Hamlet may be drawn by what seems to be his father's ghost

> to the dreadful summit of the cliff
> That beetles o'er his base into the sea ...
> The very place puts toys of desperation,
> Without more motive, into every brain
> That looks so many fathoms to the sea
> And hears it roar beneath.

Many people in the first shock of grief will resonate with these lines. Even away from these opening extremities we have a constant sense of the gulf between the grieving and other people living their *normal lives*. When Claudius urges Hamlet to put off his black mourning clothes, Hamlet immediately contrasts the outer public image and the inner private grief.

> But I have that within which passeth show;
> These but the trappings and the suits of woe.

Thereafter, as we know, death stalks the play and Hamlet, who has lost his father, is joined in grief by Ophelia whose father Polonius has been accidentally killed by Hamlet himself. Later in the play, in the scene referred to above, (Act IV, Scene V), Ophelia, doubly shocked first by the break-up of her relationship with Hamlet and then by the sudden murder of her father, enters 'distracted, with her hair down playing on a lute'. Moving between the King and Queen, Ophelia sings a ballad that strangely mingles pilgrimage and death:

> How should I your true love know
> From another one?
> By his cockle hat and staff,
> And his sandal shoon.

4

The 'cockle hat and staff' are the emblems of a pilgrim leaving the familiar to set off on his holy journey. But the next verse makes it clear that his pilgrimage is through the grave and gate of death and across that dark river. Indeed, the three verses themselves map setting off on this side of the brink, the crossing into death and then for us, all that is left on the other side:

> He is dead and gone, lady,
> He is dead and gone;
> At his head a grass-green turf,
> At his heels a stone.

> White his shroud as the mountain snow,
> Larded with sweet flowers
> Which bewept to the grave did go
> With true-love showers.

The song has surely come to Ophelia in response to grief for her father, and the flowers on the grave make their own suggestions and carry specific meanings in her distracted mind. First she associates the flowers with love, and sings another song about St Valentine's Day and a ruined maiden. But then the thought of her father's death returns and she speaks in plain prose, a jumbled sentence oscillating between hope and despair, longing for aloneness and night, a strange ambiguous mix that every mourner will recognise.

> I hope all will be well. We must be patient: but I cannot choose but weep, to think they should lay him i' the cold ground. My brother shall know of it: and so I thank you for your good counsel. Come, my coach! Good-night, ladies; good-night, sweet ladies; good-night, good-night.

The ominous tones of these final 'good-nights' do not go unnoticed, and as Ophelia leaves Horatio goes out to keep watch on her. The tension in this scene is increased by the arrival of Laertes, Ophelia's brother, likewise grieving for his father and now fearing for his sister's sanity. And then, still in this same scene, Ophelia returns bearing armfuls of flowers and singing. Ophelia distributes her flowers, as if at a wedding, or perhaps at a funeral. She says 'There's rosemary, that's for remembrance; pray, love, remember: and there is pansies, that's for thoughts.' Then she leaves, again singing a funeral song, this time as though addressing herself:

> He never will come again.
> His beard was as white as snow,
> All flaxen was his poll,
> He is gone, he is gone,
> And we cast away moan:
> God ha' mercy on his soul!

> And of all Christian souls, I pray God. God be wi' ye.

With these words Ophelia exits the stage; it is the last time we see her. Having gone beyond the brink and edge of her father's death and of her own sanity she comes to that other brink, which Gertrude so movingly describes: 'on the pendent boughs her coronet weeds clambering to hang, an envious sliver broke ...'

Ophelia is torn between love and loss but she can still summon others to remember what is needful, so she says, 'love, remember'.

In Part 1 of this book we encounter poets on the brink, looking forward with trembling, remembering with pain and sometimes with remorse, but also glimpsing, even from the brink, as Luci Shaw does in the last poem, release and abundance beyond it.

I

In Memoriam, XIII

Alfred, Lord Tennyson

Tears of the widower, when he sees
A late-lost form that sleep reveals,
And moves his doubtful arms, and feels
Her place is empty, fall like these;

Which weep a loss for ever new,
A void where heart on heart reposed;
And, where warm hands have prest and closed,
Silence, till I be silent too.

Which weep the comrade of my choice,
An awful thought, a life removed,
The human-hearted man I loved,
A Spirit, not a breathing voice.

Come, Time, and teach me, many years,
I do not suffer in a dream;
For now so strange do these things seem,
Mine eyes have leisure for their tears;

My fancies time to rise on wing,
And glance about the approaching sails,
As tho' they brought but merchants' bales,
And not the burthen that they bring.

This passage, from early in *In Memoriam*, starts with a moment of imaginative empathy. At this stage in the poem Tennyson is still waiting, between the first news of Hallam's death and the arrival of his body. Hallam had died abroad, and until his body could be brought home to England by sea there could be no funeral. Tennyson is not a widower, but a young bachelor who has lost a friend, yet somehow his grief also teaches him to see and understand the grief of others. It is as though, waiting on the brink of a funeral that has not yet happened, he glances across at another funeral, glimpses other mourners, sees the tears, perhaps, of an older man who has lost his wife, and feels a desolate companionship even in that fall of tears:

> Tears of the widower, when he sees
> A late-lost form that sleep reveals,
> And moves his doubtful arms, and feels
> Her place is empty, fall like these;

What enables this imaginative empathy? At one level, at least, it is the gift of poetry itself – all the great English poetry in which the young Tennyson was already soaked. For in this opening verse, in which the widower has dreamt that his wife is still with him and has reached for her at night only to find her place in the bed empty, Tennyson is recalling John Milton's moving Sonnet XXIII, written on the death of his wife, which ends :

> But Oh! as to embrace me she inclin'd,
> I wak'd, she fled, and day brought back my night.

Just as the memory of Milton's poetry enlarged Tennyson's sympathies, so it may be that the many poems of love and lament in these pages will enlarge ours.

The next verse opens out what it is that both Tennyson and his imagined widower are weeping for, and this can only be expressed in paradox and strange tense juxtaposition: 'Which weep a loss forever new'. This paradox of loss itself as something constantly renewed will be familiar to all who grieve: again and again, it seems that we stumble across our loss and it presents itself afresh. The next line takes that paradox further with the double sense of void and fullness. What could be more full than that place 'where heart on heart reposed', each full of love, yet that is precisely where there is now a 'void'. Just as 'heart on heart' is juxtaposed to 'void' so 'warm hands' are coupled in contrast with 'silence'. In one sense Tennyson is still describing the widower in his empty bed, yet he is also expressing his own tender grief for Hallam.

In the third verse Tennyson speaks directly of Hallam as 'the comrade of my choice', 'the human-hearted man I loved'. Here the contrast is between the warm, breathing, physically embodied person we have loved and the seemingly remote abstraction of 'a Spirit'; like the widower, Tennyson has to learn, again and again, most bitterly, that this is not a dream: it has really happened, and so he makes a strange prayer to time itself:

> Come, Time, and teach me, many years,
> I do not suffer in a dream;

At one level he is asking Time to teach him only one lesson – to learn that 'this is real' – but there is a greater reach and resonance in the ringing rhyme, 'Come, Time, and teach me, many years'. For the coming years will indeed have many things to teach Tennyson: not simply that his loss is real, but that his love is not given in vain or wasted. Some wisdom and fruit of his having loved and lost will be with him in the future and, of course, for all the readers of his poem.

This section of *In Memoriam* ends with another pair of contrasts: this time between tears that fall and fancies that rise.

> Mine eyes have leisure for their tears;

> My fancies time to rise on wing,
> And glance about the approaching sails,
> As tho' they brought but merchants' bales,
> And not the burthen that they bring.

Here Tennyson is trying to make the best of this dreadful interval between the death and the funeral as he waits for the ship to bring Arthur's body home. Time then to weep but also time for the imagination to 'rise on wing'. And so in the last verse he imagines seeing the approaching sails. He knows that some people will see the approaching ship as simply bringing 'merchants' bales' but, he, as he sees it in his mind's eye, knows that it carries the far more precious freight of his belovèd, whom at this point he can scarcely bear to name. And so he refers to the body, in a strange and tender veiling 'the burthen that they bring'. 'Burthen' here is a very powerful word; the deliberately archaic rendering of 'burden' gives an aura of decorum and beauty but still carries its double sense of the burden of the body itself and burden of grief that Tennyson's soul bears as surely as the ship bears its physical burden. For Tennyson, and also for Hallam, there may have been a further specifically poetic sense of the word, for in poetry and song the 'burden' is the returning refrain – sometimes the concluding rhyme, in ballads often a lament.

At the core of Tennyson's passionate friendship with Arthur Hallam was their common love of poetry. Hallam was especially interested in its structure, form and rhyme. In a work about the influence of Italian poetry published in his own lifetime, Hallam had made the brilliant comment that all rhyme is a parlay between memory and hope. When the first, as yet unrhymed end-word comes, part of our pleasure is in the hope and anticipation of the rhyme word that will come later to confirm or complete it. And when that rhyme word does come, our pleasure in it consists in remembering the first unrhymed word, which it couples and completes. This pleasure is at its simplest and most obvious in rhyming couplets, rhyming AA, BB and so on; more subtle rhyme schemes increase the tension and postpone the pleasure of completion, the satisfaction of hope. For this poem Tennyson invented a rhyme scheme that includes that delay. All the quatrains of *In Memoriam* rhyme ABBA. It is as though the initial A couplet has been opened out and expanded and we must pass first through the small satisfaction of the B couplet before we come to the completion, the returning A sound for which we have been waiting. In that inner couplet the intervening time may have much to teach us.

As it is with each stanza so it is with the overarching structure of *In Memoriam* itself. The poem opens with the words, 'Strong son of God, Immortal Love'; the work begins with a glimpse of the love of God behind all things. It finishes with a sense of God himself understood, not only as the Alpha of our beginning but the Omega of glory towards which we move. The last quatrain of the poem reads:

That God, which ever lives and loves,
One God, one law, one element,
And one far-off divine event,
To which the whole creation moves.

But in between this strong opening and closing, this Alpha and Omega, Tennyson sets all that time, in the intervening years, has still to teach us.

2

The Going

Thomas Hardy

Why did you give no hint that night
That quickly after the morrow's dawn,
And calmly, as if indifferent quite,
You would close your term here, up and be gone
Where I could not follow
With wing of swallow
To gain one glimpse of you ever anon!

Never to bid good-bye
Or lip me the softest call,
Or utter a wish for a word, while I
Saw morning harden upon the wall,
Unmoved, unknowing
That your great going
Had place that moment, and altered all.

Why do you make me leave the house
And think for a breath it is you I see
At the end of the alley of bending boughs
Where so often at dusk you used to be;
Till in darkening dankness
The yawning blankness
Of the perspective sickens me!

You were she who abode
By those red-veined rocks far West,
You were the swan-necked one who rode
Along the beetling Beeny Crest,
And, reining nigh me,
Would muse and eye me,
While Life unrolled us its very best.

Why, then, latterly did we not speak,
Did we not think of those days long dead,
And ere your vanishing strive to seek
That time's renewal? We might have said,
'In this bright spring weather
We'll visit together
Those places that once we visited.'

If Tennyson had to imagine the 'tears of a widower', then
Thomas Hardy gives us those tears themselves in this poem
written shortly after the death of his wife Emma in November
1912. Though Hardy is more famous for his great novels, he
saw himself chiefly as a poet, and although he did not publish his
first volume of poetry until 1898, when he was in his late fifties,
in his last years he published nothing but poetry. His innova-
tive verse forms, his powerful and somehow transfigured use of
ordinary language and his searing honesty had a great influence
on the poetry of the twentieth century as it developed. When
Philip Larkin, deeply influenced by Hardy, came to compile the
Oxford Book of Twentieth Century English Verse, it included
more of Hardy's verse than Eliot's.

'The Going' voices a widower's feelings and desperate ques-
tions standing just on the other side of the immediate brink of
death itself. The belovèd has gone and he feels he had no warning
of her going, no time to prepare or to say goodbye. Three of the
five verses begin with the question 'Why', all of them addressed,
it would seem, both poignantly and pointlessly, to Emma herself.

Indeed, the very alternation of the opening words of the verses express, by themselves, that shuttling movement between shock, disbelief and confusion: 'Why ... Never ... Why ... You ... Why'. We will come in a moment to the particular circumstance that gave rise to this poem, but in one sense it is universal. Hardy voices everyone's experience on this brink, all the unanswered questions, all the 'if onlys', the desperate fantasy of alternative scenarios, and finally the sheer sense of loss of meaning as the question 'why' is always on our lips and always unanswered. The poem opens in language that is plain, bleak and unforgettable:

Why did you give no hint that night
That quickly after the morrow's dawn,
And calmly, as if indifferent quite,
You would close your term here, up and be gone
Where I could not follow
With wing of swallow
To gain one glimpse of you ever anon!

Those words, 'calmly ... indifferent ... close your term ... up and be gone', so final, so matter of fact, are like a slap in the face. But it is a strange paradox that we can be so hurt by the departure of those we love that we almost accuse them of bleak indifference for having gone where we cannot follow. Yet the poet wants to follow and reaches, as Tennyson did, for the image of a swallow's flight; the first stanza ends with the idea, almost of one swallow following another as it becomes just a retreating and occasionally glimpsed image.

In the second stanza Hardy expresses the particular pain felt by anyone whose belovèd dies in their absence or unexpectedly: that of not having said a proper goodbye. Now the bleak language of the first verse is modulated to the tenderness of 'lip me the softest call ... utter a wish for a word'. The tenderness of the imagined farewell, in all its softness like a vanishing dream, is contrasted with the plain morning, which he sees 'harden upon the wall'. Hardy appears to have been ignorant and elsewhere on the morning of her death, unmoved and unknowing that the

moment had come and the verse finishes with those two power-
ful and all encompassing words that sum up the effect of death:
'altered all'. The very sound of 'al' in 'altered' is pulled into the
ubiquitous black gravitation of 'all'.

Then comes another almost universal experience, the trick of
the eye, the mocking memory, which makes us think that we
have seen the belovèd in some familiar place where one would
expect to see her. And, of course, when the illusion vanishes, the
place is more desolate than ever. Hardy expresses that sickening,
giddying jolt of loss perfectly:

> Till in darkening dankness
> The yawning blankness
> Of the perspective sickens me!

The fourth verse brings a change in tone, the relief and brief
blessing of deeper memory, as Hardy looks back over 40 years
to the early 1870s when he had courted Emma in Cornwall amid
the 'red-veined rocks' of the 'far-West' where they rode horses
together, she in her 'swan-necked' beauty riding by him. He
remembers how she

> reining nigh me,
> Would muse and eye me,
> While Life unrolled us its very best.

This is a picture of Emma in her prime, in control, both of herself
and of the relationship, for it is surely not just the horse she
reins, but something of Hardy's life and feeling too. The word
'muse' also does not fall idly from a poet's lips. At one level she
is musing upon him, eyeing him in a sense that has an erotic
charge, but she is also being and becoming his muse, a role she
clearly resumes at her death. As so often with Hardy, it is the
final verse that deepens, clarifies, and in some sense rereads the
whole poem:

Why, then, latterly did we not speak,
Did we not think of those days long dead,
And ere your vanishing strive to seek
That time's renewal?

Up until now we might have thought we were reading a poem
by someone who had just lost a wife who had always been the
tenderest and most belovèd, but here Hardy confesses, frankly
and with self-reproach, that it was not so, and indeed it wasn't.
In the last 20 years of their marriage Hardy and Emma had
become almost completely estranged. She had been disturbed by
the growing darkness and bleakness of his fatalist atheism, espe-
cially as expressed in his final novel, *Jude the Obscure*, which
she also feared contained, obliquely, an unflattering portrait of
their marriage. She had sought isolation, living almost alone
in the attics she had asked him to make for her, while he had
ceased to open his heart to hers and instead sought consolation
in friendships with other women. Then she died. And suddenly,
powerfully, bitterly and too late, the full force of his early love
returned to Hardy, and with it a realisation of what a poor
husband he had been. Indeed, among the papers in Emma's attic
bedroom he found a notebook entitled, 'What I Think of My
Husband'. When he read it he was seared to the core. The note
he put on the wreath on her graveside read, 'From her lonely
husband with old affection'. What honesty and power was in
those words 'old affection', but out of this experience, and not
sparing himself, Hardy crafted the great poems of 1912–13, of
which this is the first, giving a voice – honest, purgative, but
ultimately healing – to grief and regret.

We need poems like this because when someone dies it is not
just the good times and the untroubled love that we remember. It
is also the hurt, the brokenness, the wounds we have given and
taken. There is so much unfinished business, so much still to be
healed and reconciled. We are fortunate indeed if we have had
a chance to be reconciled, to make peace, to say our goodbyes,
before a person dies. If that has not happened, if death has cut
off a conversation in mid-flow and left things unresolved, then

we have to try – in poetry, in dreams, and above all in prayer – to finish the work ourselves, to say what needed saying and pray for peace both for ourselves and for the departed. Hardy did not have the consolation and resource of a Christian faith and so these tragic yet beautiful poems are his attempt both to confess his fault and to make peace with Emma. But if we have faith then we can take all that is still hurting and unresolved and offer it to God in prayer, knowing that the one we see no longer is in God's presence. We can ask that something of the peace and reconciliation he offers them in his presence may come to us too as we continue our lives. Paradoxically the poetry of this great and honest atheist may help us to do just that.

3

Lucencies

Michel Faber

Sometimes, the way words sound
Is perfect for the thing they name.
Sometimes, to our shame, they let us down.
'Love', for which we should have found
the most melodious breath of air
such as we gave to 'cashmere' or to 'share',
is like a dog's annoying bark, a bore,
'Love! Love! Love! Love!' – until the creature tires
and falls asleep, or we aren't listening anymore.
And as for 'wife' – another canine yelp,
'Wife! Wife! Wife! Wife' – a yapping yelp
ignored behind a door.
Whoever thought up 'body' for our fleshly form
was plainly not inspired by tenderness or awe.
A dodgy vehicle, this word, comedic, shoddy.

And yet, sometimes, the opposite applies:
horror is wrapped in euphony.
Vicious words that sweetly sing.
What a rich, delicious thing
'myeloma' sounds, a grand indulgence,
this cancer mulling in the bone.
Muted, subtle in its onset,
Each darling little cell a 'clone', a harmony
of dark biology, labouring in concert,

its reasoning unknown.
'Death', so soft and moth-like, delicate
as gossamer. And how pretty 'loss' and 'frail';
how dulcet 'chemotherapy' and 'fail'.

Most beautiful of all are those pale glows
revealed by radiography.
'Lucencies'. Surprise! Surprise!
Resembling fireflies,
These ghostly holes embedded in your skull,
your humerus, your pelvis and your spine.
The scans and dyes allow each one to shine.

Michel Faber is best known as a writer of lucid and beautiful
prose: essays, short stories, evocative fables and powerful novels,
but in 2016 he published an extraordinary book of poetry called
Undying: a Love Story. These poems, read in sequence, tell
the story of his love for his wife Eva, of their journey together
through the cancer that eventually killed her and of Michel's
grief as a widower. Though most of the poems were written after
Eva's death, the first part of the book is set in the time of her
illness; the second part is an account of the poet's inner life after
her death.

This poem is the first of two that I have chosen for this anthol-
ogy, both called 'Lucencies'; the second, which we will come to in
Part 6, is the poem that concludes *Undying*. The way that second
poem helps us to remember and reread the first will be part of the
final meaning of this first poem. But for now it is important to
read this poem simply on its own, not yet illuminated by the one
that is to come, just as in life we must go through the traumas of
grief unaided even though subsequent insights may help us to see
hidden lights in what we have suffered.

The poem starts with a poet's sensitivity to sound. Indeed,
this poem is particularly euphonious, beautiful sounding. Listen
to the assonance of those opening lines, not just the chiming

rhymes of 'sound' and 'down' but the playful echoes in each line of the 'ay' sounds: 'way', 'name', 'shame', 'they'. The purpose of these first sentences is to draw the contrast between profound and beautiful things and the sometimes brief and unsatisfactory words that summon them. So 'love', which should be a 'most melodious breath of air', is like 'wife', a short, barking syllable; and 'body', which should suggest all the variety and beauty of our form, is simply made to rhyme, comically, with 'shoddy'. This first stanza is more than just a lament for the inadequacy of some words, for the three words it holds up and wishes were fairer are the three that take us to the core of the tragedy: love, wife and body. All the depth of love, all the complex intimacy between husband and wife, shockingly, shoddily collide with the random brokenness and frailty of a particular body.

And then the second stanza poignantly turns the problem the other way around, observing how strangely, inappropriately beautiful are many words associated with disease and death. How much horror, as the poet strikingly says, is 'wrapped in euphony'. It was a myeloma that Eva was suffering from, and so the irony with which Faber sees the word itself as 'rich, delicious' and indulgent is almost unbearable. Then come the words he chooses to describe the growth of the cancer, taking their form and cue from the previous lines, so we get the cancer 'mulling in the bone', as though a poet were mulling over a word in his mind, or a genial host mulling wine in a kitchen.

It is hard to know the tone in which to read the lines:

Each darling little cell a 'clone', a harmony
of dark biology, labouring in concert,
its reasoning unknown.

And then this second verse broaches the word that no one wants to use, the word that even undertakers so studiously avoid:

'Death', so soft and moth-like, delicate
as gossamer. And how pretty 'loss' and 'frail';
how dulcet 'chemotherapy' and 'fail'.

Again, Faber is using all his skill as a poet to bring out these lucid ironies of beauty in the sheer mellifluous flow of vowel sounds: 'soft ... moth-like ... gossamer'. There is a deeper irony still when we read this poem in the wider context of all the other love poems to Eva in Faber's book, for it is not just these words but Eva herself who was 'delicate', 'soft', 'pretty', 'dulcet', 'most beautiful of all'. It is as though the words themselves are taking on the beauty of the woman they have taken away.

But these first two stanzas, reflecting on language itself, are really preparing us for the final focus in the third stanza on the word that gives the poem its title. 'Lucencies', as Faber tells us, is a technical term. He speaks of them as 'those pale glows revealed by radiography', a phrase that is as powerful for what it doesn't say as for what it does, for the pale glow of the lucency reveals the active presence of the cancer. And yet nothing can rob the word 'lucency' of its beauty or the promise of hope implicit in the very idea of light. In one sense all the poems in Faber's book (and, I hope, all the poems in this book too) are lucencies, points of light that reveal or clarify something otherwise hidden or obscured. In the final lines of this poem, with fearful honesty, Faber faces what these 'lucencies' mean: they are 'ghostly holes', both visually in the sense of that pale shine on an X-ray and more deeply with the sense that the word 'ghostly' brings of impending death and the way the word 'holes', speaks both of the effect of the cancer on Eva's body and also anticipates the coming sequence of 'ghostly holes', stabbing glimpses of nothingness and absence that strike all the bereaved. Yet this poem, so sensitive to the summoning aura of every word, does not end with a word like 'ghost' or 'hole' or 'death', but much more powerfully with the word 'shine'. We have to wait – and Faber shows us in his book how agonisingly long he had to wait – but there does come a time when even from these ghostly absences a new light can shine and we can discover, at last, another sense to the word 'lucencies'.

4

Their Parting

Nicholas Worskett

As our train came in late
I had not expected much
until the woman boarded with her bag,
leaving her daughter, frantic, on the platform,

desolate.

We waited far too long,
after she had closed the door:

that intermission when inaction
is forced, and all there is
is the person waiting,
and the person waited for.

The mother was busy with seating,
then the finding of her book;

her daughter, simply, beside herself:

our train not moving.

They settled into stasis,
with this conundrum of parting,
the mother busy with her purse:
both wanting it done,
and wanting it undone,
if only it could be helped:

a rehearsal for something similar,
but much, much worse.

There was nothing left, but waving.

The daughter mouthed
'I love you', over and over,
in an ecstasy of mime;

but her mother shrugged it all away,
as if to say, 'I'm going. Going.
Perhaps you owe me this, anyway.'
The last thing she wanted
was any fuss.

At last our train moved off,
and the daughter ran
as if to keep up with us,
as if she might hold us back:

I wanted it to stop.

And when her mother stood
and reached out one last wave:
she let it go at that.

It seemed too late;
too soon for caring.

*

For miles, I watched the mother sit
with closed eyes;
I watched her
put her book aside.

I watched her,

for one whole hour –
one whole hour –

staring.

There is something about being in transit that makes us detached observers. Perhaps it is the sense that we will never see the people again that allows us to observe and speculate so much about the lives of strangers we see on railway platforms and in trains, or in airport departure lounges. A long train journey, in particular, brings us a seemingly endless sequence of glimpses of other people's lives as they board and leave the train. This common experience is the starting point for Nicholas Worskett's poignant poem, but as he witnesses, and allows us to witness, the parting of a mother and daughter, we find that in some sense it is not just the mother who has boarded the train and will journey for that long hour in the poet's company; we are on board too. Somehow this parting has become, in the poet's deft and understated reference to death, 'a rehearsal'; and it is the same for us, and for the poet too: a rehearsal, a glimpse, a premonition.

One of the ways this poem succeeds is by its deliberately ordinary 'untransfigured' language, its commonplace images of late trains, carriage windows, a book, a bag, a purse, a last wave. But gradually and all by subtle implication we find that every gesture – the bag, the purse with which the mother feigns to be so busy – is packed full with intimations of mortality, with the elegiac undertow of life, the finality of parting. There is wonderful observation and insight in the contrasts between mother and daughter: 'daughter, frantic ... beside herself' ... mouthing 'I love you', in an 'ecstasy of mime', running after the moving train. There there is the stoic, perhaps embarrassed mother, wanting to play it down, to deflect and distract from it: 'busy with seating ... finding of her book ... busy with her purse ... shrugged it away' – but at the end standing and reaching out for 'one last wave'. Just in these little vignettes of a parting, Worskett seems to disclose the story of an entire relationship. One can imagine a lifetime of that mother and daughter, so different from one another, often getting on each other's nerves, embarrassing one another, misunderstanding one another, one always overstating things and the other never saying enough; and yet, underneath it all, deeply loving one another. Now, in the poignancy of parting, that buried love rises wordlessly and too late to the surface.

But we are on the train too:

We waited far too long,
after she had closed the door:

that intermission when inaction
is forced, and all there is
is the person waiting,
and the person waited for.

These limpid, inclusive lines are surely as much about all of us
as they are about this mother and daughter. At one level, 'We
waited far too long, after she had closed the door' is directly
about this train, about the embarrassment of its not moving
immediately off, of the way it forces the mother and daughter
to face one another on either side of the isolating glass, the way
it imposes on them an intermission of inaction. But surely there
is another sense in which all of us are forced, especially in the
unpredictably long, last hours of dying, to wait with and on and
for one another. Anyone sitting by a bedside or waiting in the
wings of a ward will know that forced inaction, that terrible
sense in which the world contracts and 'all there is is the person
waiting, and the person waited for'. Indeed, this poem takes us
deep into the core of what the poet memorably calls the 'conun-
drum of parting', and that conundrum is an unbearable place to
be, something the poet confesses, and allows us to confess, in an
aptly isolated sentence: 'I wanted it to stop.' The placement of
this line in the poem is brilliant. It comes just after the train has
finally started moving and the daughter is beginning to run along
the platform to stay abreast with her mother: so in one sense
we could read this line as saying that we want the train to stop;
certainly that is what the daughter wants, and perhaps it is what
the mother secretly wants too. But we know that it is not just the
train we want to stop. It is this whole awful business, not just of
their parting, but of our parting, of our inevitable parting from
one another at some station in life, somewhere: that parting for
which every other parting is a rehearsal. We want it to stop, we

want time to stop. And perhaps there is something in the experience of love, something at the core of loving itself, that promises us that it will: that time will not so much stop as be transcended. We all know these transcendent moments, and they are often moments of parting, looking into a person's eyes and knowing that there is something of 'for ever' in the moment as it passes. Shakespeare put it well in one of his sonnets: after so much about the fleetingness of time, after confessing that 'summer's lease has all too short a date', he nevertheless asserts that 'thy eternal summer shall not fade'. But for now, like the poet on the train, like the mother and the daughter, all of us are caught in an 'in between' time; forced to wait between 'too late' and 'too soon'.

5

Another Kiss

Scott Cairns

Far sweeter as a greeting, this parting
of lips became the concluding gesture
love would bear between my father and me.
In this last hour of his death his fever
had retreated so that as my kiss found
the smooth passage of his neck, I felt
how the cold surprise was beginning there.

And so we waited, and I kept my sight
fixed upon his face, which worked with less
conviction – which appeared to acquiesce.
I studied his preference for fainter effort:
the softening of his brow, the rounding
edges and, as if he could speak, the slight
movement of his lips, nearly opening.

All of this, so I would remember the hour
and the moment of my father's death,
so I might rehearse the silent language
of this final speech. His lungs were filling
and gave him less and less reason to breathe.
Lifting briefly, his lips in the semblance
of a kiss, and a kiss, a third kiss, he was gone.

If Nicholas Worskett's poem focuses, unflinchingly, on the difficulties inherent in 'the conundrum of parting', then Scott Cairns' restrained yet lucid account of his last moments with his father shows us that even within that conundrum love can make a place, however wordlessly, for grace and love.

> Far sweeter as a greeting, this parting
> of lips became the concluding gesture
> love would bear between my father and me.

These opening lines show us so much of what poetry, as a richer and more intentional way of using language, can offer us, especially in the way the poet works with the tension between the sentence and the line as units of meaning. If we take the first line simply in itself, there is something epigrammatic and universal. Cairns is playing with and replying to that well worn phrase 'parting is such sweet sorrow' and pushing back to say that the parting would be sweeter as a greeting. The very sounds in 'sweet' and 'greet', reach out to meet each other and clasp at the beginning of the line. But then, as the sentence flows on, beyond the line, the parting becomes not our general parting but the particular parting of lips, the last movements of his father's body, the concluding gesture of the love between father and son. It is interesting that it is the word 'love' that is doing all the work in this sentence. Love bears the gesture between father and son, and rightly so, for it is only love that bears all things. And there is even more suggested as 'bear' becomes 'bear between'; it is almost as though love itself has become a figure who both bears a burden and bears messages, gestures, back and forth, between father and son. The opening phrase of the second sentence in this first stanza also summons something otherwise invisible; gently the words 'this last hour of his death' summons the familiar phrase in the Ave Maria: 'Pray for us, now and at the hour of our death.' The stanza finishes with the son's farewell kiss, itself a messenger or servant of love. It is the kiss, rather than the poet, that finds the 'smooth passage'. The poet brings himself in only at the end of this first stanza, when he speaks obliquely of death as it begins in the body as the 'cold surprise'.

Like 'Their Parting', this poem is about waiting for an uncertain time and about what can be said without words. The whole second stanza conveys that concentrated and loving attention the poet gives his father. There are no histrionics, nothing 'frantic', as there was for the daughter on the platform, but a kind of concentrated stasis, all suggested in those beautifully chosen present continuous verbs: 'softening ... rounding ... opening'.

After the intense close-up of the first two verses, the final verse opens us out to a different perspective; even in the present moment of his waiting with his father at and for the hour of his death, the poet is casting forward to the time when this will be memory:

All of this, so I would remember the hour
and the moment of my father's death,

Cairns reaches for the same word that Worskett uses: 'rehearse'. But in Worskett's poem it is a dreadful, helpless and somehow imposed 'rehearsal'; for Cairns, the deliberate, quiet attention to his father looks towards a different kind of rehearsal, not so much an anticipation, as a loving restatement and invocation, a rehearsal in which the living might articulate something on behalf of the dying:

so I might rehearse the silent language
of this final speech.

There is no aversion of the eyes from the dying itself, no fumbling with purses or bags. He sees the fatal process: 'His lungs were filling', but not with air – a filling that gives him 'less reason to breathe'. Cairns gives complete attention to his father's final gesture, which is at once a semblance and utterly clear truth:

Lifting briefly, his lips in the semblance
of a kiss, and a kiss, a third kiss, he was gone.

There is something in the rhythmic, repetitive simplicity of that final line that gives each and every word of one syllable the sense of a graceful, final tolling bell.

In his poem 'The Hospital', Philip Larkin, lamenting the strange impersonal sealed isolation of hospital wards, speaks of what he calls 'the costly aversion of the eyes from death', and in some ways Nicholas Worskett's poem also observes that evasion and embarrassment. By contrast, Scott Cairns' poem gives us an intimate glimpse of how, with quietness and dignity, we can face and out-face death by daring to be face to face with one another when it happens.

6

Harbouring Christ

Frances Ward

With them he'd stop, let go, begin to laugh,
Dissolving stain, the strain: time and again.
Until this time when nothing was enough
To harbour him who bore all grief and sin.
Foreboding, deep as death, tore at their heart:
Relentless image of his body speared:
Juice of life and blood outpoured. His part
He had to play despite the end they feared.
Against the taste of death, a fragrance strong.
Those lovely feet were soothed with tears and oil,
Perfumed and dried, that soon would bear him on.
Her long red hair held scent of him, from coil
To length, through pain of days and time when much
Was gone of love, and he beyond her touch.

Like Scott Cairns' 'Another Kiss', Frances Ward's poem is about taking the time and courage to say goodbye to someone just before they die; to be with them and to bear with them, to try to express love, even as the chance of doing so in this world seems to be coming to an end. 'Harbouring Christ' also takes us into the heart of Holy Week, to the days before Good Friday. The poem is set in the house at Bethany where Mary, Martha and Lazarus harboured Christ, giving him their quiet hospitality and tokens of love in a brief retreat amid all the emotion and drama of Passiontide. The poem, beautifully cast as a traditional Shakespearean sonnet, opens with the perspective of all three members of the Bethany household:

> With them he'd stop, let go, begin to laugh,
> Dissolving stain, the strain: time and again.

These lines gently suggest that the house at Bethany has often been a sanctuary and retreat for Jesus:

> Until this time when nothing was enough
> To harbour him who bore all grief and sin.

There is a paradoxical turn here, as the Bethany household, who are trying to do their bit to take the weight off Jesus' shoulders, realise that it is indeed he who is bearing 'all grief and sin', including their own. The key word in this fourth line is 'harbour': in its implicit nautical metaphor it carries the idea of a safe haven, the port in a storm that Mary, Martha and Lazarus are hoping to provide. Indeed, the assonance in the phrase 'harbour him who bore all grief' almost has the sense of Christ as the vessel taking shelter in that harbour, deeply freighted with all the grief of humankind, bearing the weight of grief in its hold. The word 'harbour' also foreshadows the accusation Mary, Martha and Lazarus are risking: they are 'harbouring' a criminal. And there is a third importance to the word 'harbour', an allusion to another, later act of gentle sheltering to which we will turn at the end of this reflection.

In the second quatrain we feel that we are focusing on Mary's personal premonition of Christ's death, which leads her to the 'beautiful, useless gesture'* of his anointing:

> Foreboding, deep as death, tore at their heart:
> Relentless image of his body speared:
> Juice of life and blood outpoured.

---

* A phrase from my poem XIV in the sequence 'Stations of the Cross'.

The vivid, almost shocking, image of 'Juice of life and blood outpoured' may be an allusion to George Herbert's poem 'The Agony', which asks us 'to assay and taste that juice which on the cross a pike did set again abroach'. Herbert, anticipating the Eucharist, already sees the blood outpoured as the eucharistic wine; as he says at the end of his poem:

Love is that liquor sweet and most divine,
Which my God feels as blood and I as wine.

Returning to Ward's poem, a key word in line 7 is 'outpoured'. It is out of her foreboding of the blood to be outpoured so generously for us that Mary pours out so generously the precious ointment, described in a beautiful line, 'Against the taste of death, a fragrance strong.'

Like Nicholas Worskett's 'Their Parting', this poem is about a kind of rehearsal for the parting of death, but whereas in that railway station encounter everything was left unsaid, here Mary is able fully to express her love. She has 'soothed with tears' those 'lovely feet' which 'soon would bear him on' into the Passion. Notice the gentle insistence, again, on the word 'bear'. And there is a mutuality and exchange in the encounter. Just as she perfumes his feet, so too

Her long red hair held scent of him, from coil
To length, through pain of days and time when much
was gone of love, and he beyond her touch.

The gentle way in which these lines suggest how Mary undoes her hair and lets it down 'from coil to length', in a kind of unfolding and loosening, symbolises the whole atmosphere and ministry to Jesus of that house at Bethany, as a place of loosening, uncoiling and relaxing. But finally we must ask, is this poem just about Mary Magdalene and Jesus? Can it be about us too? About our harbouring of those we love in our homes and in our hearts before and after their death? Does it model and suggest ways in which we too can make something beautiful out of our foreboding?

Here we return to that important word harbouring. Frances

Ward, former Dean of Bury St Edmund's as well as scholar and poet, published a fine article in *Theology* in 2011 on the intimate spiritual friendship between John Donne and Lady Magdalene Herbert. She draws attention to a beautiful poem by Donne addressed to his belovèd Magdalene, which accompanied a set of sonnets about Christ's life and passion: 'La Corona'. Donne praises Magdalene as worthy of her namesake and specifically mentions the house at Bethany (or Bethina, in Donne's poem) and also Mary's role in bringing news of the resurrection. In the conclusion of the poem, Donne uses the word 'harbour' twice:

> and in some recompense
> That they did harbour Christ himself, a Guest
> Harbour these Hymns, to his dear name addresst.

Ward's understanding of this intimate friendship – of the way in which Magdalene Herbert harboured Donne in the storms of his life and how they each deepened the other's faith, their mutual harbouring of Christ – surely influenced the way she phrases her own poem. Indeed, she has written of this poem:

> It was the sensuality and intimacy of Jesus' friendship with those who lived at Bethina – and particularly with Mary Magdalene – that I tried to capture in 'Harbouring Christ'. Like Donne I wasn't too concerned about which Mary was which, or who 'they' are – the amalgamation of the Marys, or Lazarus, Martha and Mary – simply to capture Jesus harboured in intimacy and trust, with passionate love, as all anticipate the passion to which he was called and couldn't escape, and through which he would be borne by a love that was expressed by the passionate intimacy that he knew with his friends and which was of God.

The suggestion here, surely, is that just as the parting of Mary Magdalene and Christ became a pattern for Magdalene Herbert and Donne, so too the contemplation of that moment in the house at Bethany can deepen and enrich our own friendships and our partings.

7

To What End This First and Final Life?

Luci Shaw

Sewing up the seams as words
grow into sentences, verbs don't fit,
fall into place. Nothing proceeds
according to plan. There isn't a plan.
I perform confusion instead of composition.

Ivy, wanton, creeps up the wall,
against my will, tendrils shading
my window. I write in a kind of
stippled shadow. The oriental rug
with its intricate colors – pear green
woven with crimson and copper –
darkens with the onset of night.

To what end this first and final life?
When I surrender I pray the world will
reach out, take me in, grow me
as something new. The wheat field
flashes its gold invitation:
Grow now, flourish, and in good time
release abundance – a new crop.

To end this first section on 'Brinks and Edges' we have a poem in which the poet herself contemplates coming to the brink of her own life. The distinguished American poet Luci Shaw, born in 1928 and author of over ten collections of poetry celebrating the beauty of nature and reflecting on every phase and stage of our Christian pilgrimage, is still writing great verse. In this new poem, not yet published or collected but kindly shared with me for this anthology, she writes with paradoxical clarity about the struggles and confusions with language itself that old age sometimes brings, and yet in her gentle and understated way she also hints at the growth and gift hidden in the apparent finality of our mortal life.

The first verse opens with a sense of growth and yet of something uncontained. 'Sewing up the seams as words grow', as 'verbs don't fit', almost suggests a mother having to remake her children's clothes as they grow out of them, and in one sense that is the experience of every poet. With words we try to make a garment to clothe experience and insight, but it never quite fits; life always outgrows the clothing of our expression. But in another sense, the context and title of this poem suggest the experience of frustration when we cannot find the right word, when loss of memory and confusion make it so hard to say what we mean, to make or keep a plan, when we end up performing 'confusion instead of composition'.

This sense of age creeping up on us, covering or overshadowing what was once clear, is taken up in the image that opens the second stanza, with the wanton ivy creeping up the wall 'against my will', its 'tendrils shading my window'. 'I write in a kind of stippled shadow' is at once a beautiful, natural, closely observed image, the hallmark of Luci's poetry, and a quiet, understated emblem of the difficulties of taking up the task again at an advanced age. She looks at the carpet in her room and sees its intricate colours, all the rich and particular details of our sensory life in this body, darkening 'with the onset of night', and asks the key question: 'To what end this first and final life?'

A poet without Christian hope might have ended the poem there, and all of us, whether Christian or not, could have identified with the experience she describes, the question she asks. But Luci chooses to end her poem not with a question but with a prayer. Hidden in that prayer, indeed forming its very substance, is a deeper understanding of the word 'end'. 'End' can simply mean termination: the end of a day, the end of a sentence, the end of a life. But it can also mean purpose and fulfilment. We do something with a particular end in view, a particular purpose. The end a poet has in view is not simply the last word, but the purpose of the poem: to offer a fleeting glimpse, a clarification, a vision that transcends the words and images of which the poem is composed.

The question with which Luci closes the first two stanzas and opens the third is one about purpose and meaning as well as mere mortality. She answers her question with a prayer that is at once a gracious surrender to the finality of this mortal life, to the good earth to which we will all in the end surrender our bodies, and also an affirmation of hope, a glimpse of new growth and transformation:

When I surrender I pray the world will
reach out, take me in, grow me
as something new.

We might take this at the literal level to be a prayer that our physical bodies might become part of the nourishment in good soil that is taken up by the miraculous processes of biological life, as the poppies grew in Flanders fields, but the final lines invite us to a deeper reading:

The wheat field
flashes its gold invitation:
Grow now, flourish, and in good time
release abundance – a new crop.

Hidden in these lines is a delicate allusion to Jesus' teaching about his own death and ours: 'Very truly, I tell you, unless a grain of wheat falls into the earth and dies, it remains just a single grain; but if it dies, it bears much fruit' (John 12.24).

Jesus is speaking of his death on the cross, telling the disciples that now the hour has come for the Son of Man to be glorified. In the very act of surrender, of letting go, letting the seed fall to the good earth, he is promising resurrection. Now the 'stippled shadow', the dark invitation of 'the onset of night' earlier in the poem has become a 'gold invitation', an invitation to growth and flourishing beyond the finality of this first life, and we realise the promise of more that was always hidden in that little word 'first'. As she closes the poem she makes, as it were, an unspoken wordplay. The poem opened with sewing: sewing up seams that can somehow never really contain the growth that bursts them. It ends with a positive encouragement to 'Grow now' and 'flourish', confident that there is another sowing, and a new life beyond it.

PART 2

The Shock of Loss
Calm despair and wild unrest

Introduction

In Part 1 we reflected on the difficult days leading up to death, on the rehearsals for parting, on the foreboding of the moment itself. In this second part we see how poets can describe for us – and so, perhaps, help us to get through – the actual shock and transition of the death itself, the moment when the news reaches us and we know it has happened. Here, as in each of subsequent staging posts on this journey, the lucid honesty of Tennyson's poetic grief journal *In Memoriam* may help us. In Section XVI of that poem, Tennyson puts his finger on one of the most strange and difficult things about bereavement: the mix of emotions, the inexplicable mood swings, each extreme of which can leave us feeling guilty either for feeling the mood or for not feeling its opposite:

> What words are these have fallen from me?
> Can calm despair and wild unrest
> Be tenants of a single breast,
> Or sorrow such a changeling be?
>
> Or doth she only seem to take
> The touch of change in calm or storm;
> But knows no more of transient form
> In her deep self, than some dead lake
>
> That holds the shadow of a lark
> Hung in the shadow of a heaven?
> Or has the shock, so harshly given,
> Confused me like the unhappy bark

That strikes by night a craggy shelf,
And staggers blindly ere she sink?
And stunn'd me from my power to think
And all my knowledge of myself;

And made me that delirious man
Whose fancy fuses old and new,
And flashes into false and true,
And mingles all without a plan?

'What words are these have fallen from me?' Tennyson asks in a
kind of numbed surprise as though he were a stranger to himself
and can't really account for what he has been saying. And that is
often the experience of people in the first shock of grief: one part
of their life is going on, on automatic pilot, almost as though
nothing has happened, and the other is numbed and struck dumb
by the unspeakable. One moment there is a calm despair that
does and says nothing and the next a restless desperation, rush-
ing from one thing to another as if mere busy-ness could turn
back time. Even in that frenetic activity the calm despair is still
sitting underneath, both responses are indeed, as Tennyson says
'tenants of a single breast'.

In the second and third stanzas Tennyson offers us the sugges-
tive image of a deep lake, whose surface may seem to change 'in
calm or storm' and whose surface in those calms reflects what
happens above it, even the shadow (meaning reflection here) of a
lark; but none of that changes the deep self at the bottom of what
seems like a dead lake. The choice of the word shadow rather
than reflection is also telling: the lake 'holds the shadow of a lark
hung in the shadow of a heaven'. This is not simply describing
the sky and the bird reflected in the lake's surface; it suggests that
for the bereaved, lost in the valley of the shadow of death, all
things seem somehow shadowy and insubstantial, not their real
selves. Having given us the image of the lake, he changes, per-
haps at the suggestion of water, to the image of a ship foundering
and staggering before it sinks:

Or has the shock, so harshly given,
Confused me like the unhappy bark

That strikes by night a craggy shelf,
And staggers blindly ere she sink?
And stunn'd me from my power to think
And all my knowledge of myself;

Here Tennyson may be remembering some telling lines in George
Herbert's poem 'Miserie':

A sick toss'd vessel, dashing on each thing;
Nay, his own shelf:
My God, I mean my self.

Tennyson's repetition of the rhyme on 'shelf' and 'self' suggests
that he has learnt how the calamity of grief exposes the rocks
and shoals in our own psyche that may have been covered over
and unknown in better times. Certainly, most people experi-
encing the shock of loss will entirely understand this sense of
shipwreck, of the whole vessel of one's life suddenly striking
something, shuddering and breaking apart. And then the word
'staggers' itself suggests another metaphor: that of delirium. In
the last verse Tennyson feels that he has himself become

that delirious man
Whose fancy fuses old and new,
And flashes into false and true,
And mingles all without a plan?

This section of *In Memoriam* ends with a question; indeed, these
verses are composed entirely of a series of questions: 'What
words are these ... Doth she only seem ... staggers blindly ere
she sink ... mingles all without a plan?' That in itself is a power-
ful and honest expression of the actual experience. For when we
deal with this first shock we are indeed, in some sense, stunned
out of our power to think and knowledge of ourselves. And yet,

in spite of this, Tennyson somehow writes the poem, and in so doing gives us, as we too stagger blindly, the words we need to express what we are feeling. I hope that the poems in this part acknowledge and speak into our questions, our shock and confusion, not perhaps to answer them immediately, for the deepest answer may be a longer time coming, but at least to honour them, helping us to realise that even as we feel that we are a dead lake, a sinking ship, a staggering invalid, we are not alone.

8

King John – Constance's speech

William Shakespeare

CONSTANCE
I am not mad: this hair I tear is mine;
My name is Constance; I was Geffrey's wife;
Young Arthur is my son, and he is lost!
I am not mad: I would to heaven I were!
For then, 'tis like I should forget myself:
O, if I could, what grief should I forget!
Preach some philosophy to make me mad,
And thou shalt be canonized, cardinal;
For being not mad but sensible of grief,
My reasonable part produces reason
How I may be deliver'd of these woes,
And teaches me to kill or hang myself:
If I were mad, I should forget my son,
Or madly think a babe of clouts were he:
I am not mad: too well, too well I feel
The different plague of each calamity ...

And, father cardinal, I have heard you say
That we shall see and know our friends in heaven:
If that be true, I shall see my boy again;
For since the birth of Cain, the first male child,
To him that did but yesterday suspire,
There was not such a gracious creature born.
But now will canker-sorrow eat my bud
And chase the native beauty from his cheek,

And he will look as hollow as a ghost,
As dim and meagre as an ague's fit,
And so he'll die; and, rising so again,
When I shall meet him in the court of heaven
I shall not know him: therefore never, never
Must I behold my pretty Arthur more.

CARDINAL PANDULPH
You hold too heinous a respect of grief.

CONSTANCE
He talks to me, that never had a son.

KING PHILIP
You are as fond of grief as of your child.

CONSTANCE
Grief fills the room up of my absent child,
Lies in his bed, walks up and down with me,
Puts on his pretty looks, repeats his words,
Remembers me of all his gracious parts,
Stuffs out his vacant garments with his form:
Then have I reason to be fond of grief?
Fare you well: had you such a loss as I,
I could give better comfort than you do ...
O Lord! my boy, my Arthur, my fair son!
My life, my joy, my food, my all the world!
My widow-comfort, and my sorrows' cure!

I have given quite a substantial passage from Shakespeare's *King John* as it contains so many powerful expressions and images of grief. It is not necessary to know the whole play to appreciate these words, but a little background may help.

The play is set in the reign of King John, between the death of Richard the Lionheart and John's own untimely end. All we need to know is that Prince Arthur, John's nephew – the son of his deceased elder brother – had a stronger claim to the throne than John himself, and was conveniently 'got out of the way'. Arthur was captured, then died falling from the tower in which he was imprisoned – a supposed escape attempt that was almost certainly an extra-judicial killing. This passage, in which Arthur's mother Constance confronts the loss of her son, comes at a point in the play (Act III, Scene IV) when she does not know for certain that Arthur is dead. He has been 'disappeared', and like so many mothers of the disappeared she has no body to mourn and bury. Her son is lost, but in her mother's heart she fears and somehow knows the worst.

So Shakespeare chooses this moment in his play to tackle perhaps the worst of all bereavements – the unspeakable grief of a parent who has lost a child. Some biographers think that he was drawing on his own experience of the death of his young son Hamnet when he gave these searing lines to Constance.

I chose this passage because even taken outside its context in the play it expresses three deep motifs in the experience of grief: the feeling that the bereaved sometimes have that they are going mad; the fear that whatever 'heaven' might amount to it won't be the same thing as the love that has been lost, that even if we see our belovèd in heaven they won't be recognisable; and the tormenting sense we have of the palpable, almost 'present' absence of the belovèd, the constant 'seeing' and 'remembering' them in familiar places only to find that they are not there.

At the beginning of her speech Constance confronts the question of whether she has been driven mad by the extremity of her grief, observing the unhelpful way that those around her make her feel that she is losing her sanity because they are evading the truth and wish to deny the grief she expresses. There are specific reasons for this in the plot but it also expresses the reality of our own culture: deep, fierce, dreadful grief demands a deep and dreadful expression – a proper outlet for rage as well as for lament, for despair as well as for eulogy, but we repress both. So the passage starts with Constance's bold assertion that it is in no way wrong or mad or extreme for her to feel the way she does.

And indeed she argues, quite rightly, that deep grief for those we love is a sign not of madness but of sanity:

> I am not mad: I would to heaven I were!
> For then, 'tis like I should forget myself:
> O, if I could, what grief should I forget! …
> If I were mad, I should forget my son,

Her clarity and courage here are admirable so it is all the more galling when the cardinal tells her she is overreacting: 'You hold too heinous a respect of grief.' Constance's swift and biting reply to the celibate cardinal says it all: 'He talks to me, that never had a son.' The first and only qualification for bereavement counselling is fellow feeling, common humanity, to be as vulnerable to grief yourself as the one you seek to comfort, and to admit that vulnerability.

To make it worse, the cardinal's insensitive dismissal of Constance's grief comes when she has just asked him a really important question which he completely ignores – would she recognise her son in heaven? She has asked him to unpack what he means when he tells her, 'we shall see and know our friends in heaven'; she has laid her fears before him – her fear that the sheer suffering of his end in captivity will have altered her son out of all recognition and 'he will look as hollow as a ghost'. She ends with the despairing:

> I shall not know him: therefore never, never
> Must I behold my pretty Arthur more.

And all the cardinal can reply is effectively to say 'just get over it'! He fails here entirely in the first call on any Christian, which is to be a witness to the resurrection. He could have told her that Jesus went through agony on the cross but that when he rose his friends not only knew him and loved him but saw that even the worst wounds he had suffered were somehow transfigured and glorified. He could have told her that the love Christ offered them from heaven was even stronger and more richly available to them than it had been on earth, and that we have every hope that those who die in Christ and rise with him will be like unto him, truly themselves but transposed into a richer and fuller life. He could have told her that the scars on Christ's risen body show how deeply God himself feels and will heal our wounds and grief. But no, he just ignores her question and dismisses her grief. Sadly, he is not the first or the last churchman to be guilty of this offence.

King Philip is no better: 'You are as fond of grief as of your child.' There is a play on the word 'fond' here, which was at that time a word in transition. Originally 'fond' simply meant 'mad', as when Lear describes himself as a 'very foolish fond old man'; but it also meant 'loving' in that poets, wanting to say that they were 'madly' in love, had begun to describe themselves as 'fond' of their belovèd. Then from being a statement of extreme affection the word began to settle towards its current sense of a kind of steady affection.

Philip is using 'fond' in both senses: Constance is 'fond of grief' in the sense that she is mad with grief, but also as 'fond' of it as she is fond of her child, suggesting that she has somehow transferred her affection for her child to the grief itself. Constance's robust and yet poignant reply is perhaps the single most famous passage in the whole play, and for good reason:

> Grief fills the room up of my absent child,
> Lies in his bed, walks up and down with me,
> Puts on his pretty looks, repeats his words,
> Remembers me of all his gracious parts,
> Stuffs out his vacant garments with his form:

All she has left is her grief; the grief is so much the last attachment to the child that it seems itself to take his form and yet is always a bitter reminder of his absence, summed up in that heart-rending picture of his 'vacant garments'. Surely this is also the voice of Shakespeare himself, putting into words at last his feelings at the death of his own son. Then comes Constance's dismissal of her so-called comforters:

Fare you well: had you such a loss as I,
I could give better comfort than you do

Our own grief is the only passport to the strange land of an-
other's sorrow and that is why the truest and deepest comfort
can and does come from the one who was a man of sorrows and
acquainted with grief. I can trust the promise at the end of the
Bible that God will wipe away the tears from every eye because
I know that the God who made that promise became a human
being for me, and he wept with tears like mine at the death of
his friend.

9

Grief

Elizabeth Barrett Browning

I tell you, hopeless grief is passionless;
That only men incredulous of despair,
Half-taught in anguish, through the midnight air
Beat upward to God's throne in loud access
Of shrieking and reproach. Full desertness,
In souls as countries, lieth silent-bare
Under the blanching, vertical eye-glare
Of the absolute heavens. Deep-hearted man, express
Grief for thy dead in silence like to death –
Most like a monumental statue set
In everlasting watch and moveless woe
Till itself crumble to the dust beneath.
Touch it; the marble eyelids are not wet:
If it could weep, it could arise and go.

Shakespeare gave Constance the words with which to express
her grief, but Elizabeth Barrett Browning, paradoxically, uses
her eloquence to give us a picture of grief at its most frozen and
silent. Yet her powerful sonnet does so much more than that.
She starts by involving us directly, bringing us right into the con-
versation, as though we've just told her that grief is passionate;
she reaches out, holds us by the arm and says, 'I tell you, hope-
less grief is passionless'. It's only those 'incredulous of despair',
those who haven't yet reached total despair, who still rant and

rave at God: only those who in her powerful phrase 'Half-taught in anguish' are still capable of 'shrieking and reproach'. 'Half-taught' summons an image of grief as a school, a terrible series of lessons in pain that some people never complete. No, she tells us, crying out in 'loud access' is only the shallow beginning of grief. You pass through that into something like an utterly featureless desert. And then she shows us the terrible vista of the deserted soul, for surely the image of 'Full desertness, in souls as countries,' lying 'silent-bare' under the 'vertical eye-glare of the absolute heavens' is all the more powerful for the suggestion that the desertification is also a desertion; the silent desert was once, before this shock of grief, a green and pleasant land filled not with utter silence but with the murmuring of many streams. There is a dreadful movement, too, from the first notion of a heaven that at least contained 'God's throne' – a place and a person to whom one could complain – to the impersonal 'eye-glare' of heaven so 'absolute' that one could no more appeal to it than to the punishing glare of an empty desert sky.

We feel instinctively that this is the voice of experience, and so it is. This poem was published in her two volume collection of 1844 simply titled *Poems*, under her then name E. B. Barrett. Loss and grief were the dominant themes of the whole collection and with good reason. She had been an invalid from childhood and overprotected at home, practically kept house-bound by her domineering father, but eventually a sensible doctor had said that she needed to be away from London for a while and she had a brief sojourn by the sea in Torquay. She begged her father to allow her belovèd younger brother Edward to come down and stay with her, which he did in 1840. It was good for him as well as for her. Edward took advantage of this freedom from family control and of the place to go sailing, but tragically he was drowned in a boating accident. Elizabeth's shock and grief were deepened by a terrible sense of guilt, with which she tortured herself: she had asked for him to visit, and also for him to stay longer when her father, having reluctantly let him go, was insisting on his early return. After Edward's death she returned home. She almost never left her room, while her father restricted visitors' access to her, even when she became a well-known poet whom many wanted to visit. Indeed, she was nearly chosen as Poet Laureate after the death of Wordsworth in 1850 (the laureateship went to Tennyson). No wonder she wrote to her friend Mary Russell Mitford, just after this catastrophe, 'One stroke ended my youth'.

This sonnet is about her grief for Edward. Like many sonnets, it has a 'turn' or *volta* – a point at which the sonnet turns from one mood or voice to another. Browning places her *volta* right in the middle of the eighth line. The first part ends with us trapped 'Under the blanching, vertical eye-glare of the absolute heavens'. But in the second half she addresses us again, with even more urgency and intimacy, telling us that for all the desert silence we do have something to express, in contrast to those only 'half-taught'. 'Deep-hearted man,' she says, 'express grief for thy dead in silence'. So paradoxically, for all the silence there is expression, and for all the desert isolation there is a companionship in grief with the poet; she calls us from the desert silence of her grief to express ours too, as though somehow across the white desert of the page our expressive silences are joined. And then she gives us the final, strange, telling image of the statue 'set in everlasting watch and moveless woe'. All the bereaved know that experience, that sense of having been frozen in time, turned to stone by our grief, white and chill as marble. But now, in a move of even closer intimacy, she invites us for all our desert isolation to come close and touch the marble eyelids of the statue she and we have become. Are we going to crumble into dust where we are, or is something else possible? What needs to happen to set us free? She tells us everything in her last line: 'If it could weep, it could arise and go.'

Surely in that final phrase, 'arise and go', there is an echo of Jesus' words to the paralysed man to take up his bed and walk – if only we could get to that point. Perhaps it will take the touch of another grieving person, a warm and human touch, not one of icy marble, to release the tears. And so it proved for her. Like a prince hacking through the thorns around Sleeping Beauty, another poet, Robert Browning, made his way through the thicket of paternal disapproval, and at her bedside wrought the healing of which she had despaired. She did arise and go with him, secretly, to Italy, taking with her the famous love sonnets he had inspired. And the rest, as they say, is history, but also, quite rightly, legend.

10

Earth

Malcolm Guite

Here at the graveside, holding onto earth,
The time approaches when he will let go.
But now his freezing fist is clenched as hard
As ice around the dirt of which we're made
And his poor heart is ice beneath the floe
Waiting for the moment of release.

The priest has told him that he should release
The earth he holds when he hears *earth to earth*
And dust to dust 'but just go with the flow'
He said and smiled. Instead he wants to go
A million miles from here. Why were we made
For pain like this? The flinty ground is hard

And all their breath is frosted. Frosted hard
The tears that cannot melt for their release
Wait in their frozen channels. We're unmade
By one another's deaths. We go to earth
Like animals at bay. Words come and go
But we are hiding deep beneath their flow.

So with this liturgy, its surge and flow
Seem so remote and dreamlike that it's hard
To concentrate, remember to let go
His handful of poor soil, and release
Its rattle at the coffin lid as *earth*
To earth ... remembereth whereof we are made ...

Sounds out in tones and undertones all made
Unreal, ethereal, by the easy flow
Of practised piety. Only the earth
Is silent as his heart, silent and hard
Because no words will do. 'O just release
Us into silence, finish. Let us go.'

At last it's over and he turns to go
Back to the empty house, the bed unmade,
Cards and condolences, a press release
About the accident, bereavement leaflets, flow
Over the floor. He reads: *it's always hard …*
You may be tempted just to go to earth …

Only at midnight dreams release the flow
Of frozen tears. Memory melts the hard
Heart last, and lets love go to the good earth.

There is a moving traditional ritual in the burial service in which
first the minister, and then the chief mourners, if they wish, let
fall a handful of earth onto the coffin before the mourners move
away and the gravediggers fill in the plot. It is powerful because
it involves no denial, no smoothing away, as is sometimes sug-
gested in the neat closure of curtains at a crematorium. It is
powerful because that small act of letting go is a preparation
for the larger 'letting go' that the whole funeral is helping us to
do. It is powerful but it is never easy, because however deeply
we know we have to let go we are also trying desperately to
hold on. Nevertheless, if mourners are willing to make this
beautiful gesture of loss and farewell, of emptiness and return,
I encourage them to do so. For those mourners who have been
fortunate enough to have been brought up with an awareness of
scripture, this gesture has special significance and solidarity, for
the words the priest says at this moment, 'earth to earth, ashes
to ashes, dust to dust', take us back to Genesis and the words in
which God sealed our mortality: 'from dust you were taken and

to dust you will return'. These words evoke our solidarity with one another and with the whole of humankind in our common experience of death; but that archetypal exchange in Genesis also contains a promise that the 'seed' of Eve will 'bruise the serpent's heel'. That promise was fulfilled when Christ, in complete solidarity with us, himself went down into the dust with us and there defeated death on our behalf, so that as in Adam all die, even so in Christ shall all be made alive.

But it is still a hard thing to do. At a funeral I am usually the minister intoning these words and inviting this gesture, but in this poem I have placed myself as deeply as I can into the frozen and desperate place of the bereaved person trying desperately to do the right thing and not to break down.

There is a paradox and a challenge for every minister conducting a funeral, a paradox summed up in the very word 'conduct'. In one sense I must conduct the funeral as a conductor does an orchestra, keeping everything together, helping everyone to play their part as best they can, ensuring some harmony and coherence of the parts, bringing them into a significant whole. To do that I must stand a little apart, also like a conductor. Whatever happens, I must keep myself composed and the proceedings together on behalf of those who feel themselves falling apart. But if I am to conduct a funeral well, I must be a conductor in another sense: something like a lightning conductor. The immense charge of feeling, both in the positive pole of thanksgiving and the negative pole of loss, must pass through me, and as a lightning conductor is earthed in God's good soil, so I must be rooted and grounded in love, in God himself. All the unsaid prayers, the agonies of those who have no faith and cannot pray, need to pass through me to God. My poem suggests a moment when the bereaved person feels remote from 'the easy flow of practised piety', and always, while enabling the proper flow of the service I must also somehow be open to and in solidarity with the pain. This can only be done in Christ and that is why the service is in fact one long prayer, uttered in and through Jesus.

I should say a word here about the form and original context of this poem. The poem is a sestina, a complex form in which instead of the usual variation of rhyme there is a deliberate return, stanza after stanza, to the last words of each of the first six lines. We return to these words over and over as each new stanza plays a fresh variation on their sequence: 'earth ... let go ... hard ... made ... flow ... release'. This sense of recurrent endings, of almost obsessive repetition, makes the sestina a helpful form for poems about crisis, or obsession – the constant return to things we thought we had got past – and also therefore for the experience of bereavement. But there is a redemptive possibility in all these repetitions with variation. For repetition with variation, in which each old word in a new context is somehow deepened and redeemed, is also the pattern of prayer and liturgy. In its original context, in my book *The Singing Bowl*, this poem was the fourth in a sequence of six sestinas called 'Six Glimpses', the first five of which were each about a different person in a moment of crisis. But the sixth was about a woman who happened, in the course of her day, to have glimpsed each of these five moments of crisis and suffering, and at the end of her day she returns to each moment she has seen. In prayer she lifts each person up to Christ in a kind of divine and redemptive version of the returns and repetitions in which each person was stuck. So in that final poem, titled 'Prayer', she looks back at this bereaved man she has seen at the funeral in these lines:

And then that frozen funeral ... the depths
Of grief she knows only too well. The day
Had turned so dark and wintry and her prayer
Rises on frosted breath. *Remember them*
And reach a cold man with the warmth that heals.
May he so let love go as to receive.

Open our clenched fists Heaven, to receive
The touch of mercy, mercy in the depths.
Open your wound in us, the wound that heals ...

I wanted to have some sense that the release that man experiences at the end of the poem 'Earth' was in part made possible by the prayers of a passing stranger:

> dreams release the flow
> Of frozen tears. Memory melts the hard
> Heart last, and lets love go to the good earth.

For whatever else we can do, and however inadequate we may feel in the face of another's grief, we can always pray.

11

Misunderstood in Late 20th Century Scotland

Kelly Belmonte

We borrowed space and time
in a country not our own –
before Y2K, before Columbine
and 9/11, before smart phones
and texting, before I even knew
I was Scottish – in a town dead
set between Glasgow and Edinburgh.

Took a black cab to Stirling in a
January snow, the cabbie happy
to argue with a couple of Yanks
about how Mel Gibson was no
William Wallace, though he seemed
glad enough to take our fare.

They say the Scottish speak English.
Indeed, we shared a vocabulary,
a plate of bangers and mash
spread out between us. They
mouthed fruity vowels mixed
with wool – left this American
mesmerized and without meaning.

It was hard enough, being
twenty-nine and female, stretched

thin and different – while I typed
for rent, my colleagues traded
witty quips about things
'wee' or 'brilliant' or otherwise
foreign to me. If only we
had spoken different languages.
Maybe I would have understood.

But come mid-March there was
that day of sirens. It seemed they'd
sound forever, though we knew
soon enough they would be too late
to make a difference in that
blood-filled Dunblane gymnasium:
the shared language of shock.
Then the look almost of blame,
as if I had pulled the trigger.

This would happen in America,
not here. I understood those words
perfectly – crisp, clear, nearly British
in their precision – and began to see
all that mumble-jumble accenting was
just another way to keep out
the foreign horde.

For months after, we
continued to eat
their fish and chips, walk
their craggy moors, finger
bindings in dusty bookshops,
exchange pleasantries. If anyone
mentioned Dunblane, the air
went static, the sense of shame
palpable. Little things – maybe you
asked where was home,
they might say *Dunblane.*

You wouldn't say *sorry* before
March, why say it after? So you
mouthed nothing-words –
What a quiet pretty little town,
such a nice place to live. But
your lies tasted sad. Empty.
Emptied of words. There were
not enough words in the world
to say what could not be said.

Hamilton had used his Browning pistol 105 times; 17 people were dead, 32 sustained gunshot wounds, all under just four minutes. The 106th bullet was for himself. (James Cusick, from 'Dunblane massacre: Remembering the school shooting 20 years later', *The Independent*, 10 March 2016)

This part of the book is about the 'shock of loss', and that shock, however terrible, is usually private and intimate – but not always. It seemed a good idea to find space in this anthology for that wider, shared shock, which is both intimate and public when there is a major catastrophe. Readers of my anthology *The Word in the Wilderness* will know how well the American poet Kelly Belmonte handles the personal and intimate side of prayer in her lovely poetic sequence 'How I talk to God', but in this poem, as intimate and confessional in its own way as that other sequence, she deals with the shock and sorrow we in Britain all shared, and remember, in the hideous massacre of children at Dunblane in 1996.

The first thing to note about this poem is that she doesn't name the town, doesn't mention Dunblane itself, until line 35, and when the name comes it is a shock, just as the events them-selves were; it sends us back to look at the long opening with a new eye.

The poem begins with the striking lines:

> We borrowed space and time
> in a country not our own

While the rest of the sentence makes it clear that this is a particular space, in Scotland, in a town between Glasgow and Edinburgh, at a particular time 'before' so much that has changed the world, there is a sense that those opening lines are universal; they are about all of us. Just by being alive in this world we have all, in one sense, 'borrowed space and time'. But if 'borrowed' intimates that we can only keep our space and time in this 'country not our own' for a while, perhaps that second line carries the suggestion that after we return what was borrowed here, there is, waiting for us, a country that is our own.

Belmonte makes another deft use of the interplay available in poetry between the line as a unit of sense and the longer sentence of which it is part in the line break in line 6. It is only after we have read the whole poem that we see the dark foreshadowing of the line ending – 'in a town dead' – before we pick up the primary and less sinister sense 'dead set between' in line 7. The next three verses open one of the poem's deepest themes, which is the problem of language and communication, of what it is like to be in one of 'two countries divided by a common language', as Bernard Shaw put it. But at this stage the theme is addressed in a deceptively gentle and anecdotal way.

And then comes the shock of the fifth stanza, the 'day of sirens', the poignant tension in the line that starts 'soon' and ends 'too late', and then the dreadful revelation, the naming at last of the town and the place: 'that blood-filled Dunblane gymnasium'. In that horror we return to the theme of shared or divided language, but this time it is 'the shared language of shock'.

Then immediately we are pitched into one of the most common but most destructive responses to grief: blame, the desire to push the darkness away to place it onto another. Suddenly there is 'the look almost of blame' and the assertion that '*This would happen in America, not here*', almost as though the poet, just by being an American, has opened a portal that has enabled what the British perceive as a specifically American tragedy to happen on their own soil. So the poet, as she continues her sojourn in Dunblane, feels increasingly cut off and alienated from the town even as she seeks to be more united with them in the shared language of shock and grief. But as the poem comes to its close it forces us to confront the limits of language itself, the failure of language in the face of atrocity. We, together with the poet, are left

Empty.
Emptied of words. There were
not enough words in the world
to say what could not be said.

This sense of a gap, or gulf, is further emphasised by the abrupt transition from the language of poetry, sustained over 65 lines, to the 27 bleak words of prose in the newspaper passage with which the poem concludes. We can delineate the facts but there is nothing else adequate that any of us as individuals can say. The poem ends rightly with this sense of what cannot be said; but perhaps in the opening lines, as we read them again, there is a hint of something beyond for all of us. Certainly, in that emptiness and vacuum, there is a profound desire to find in the Word, who himself suffered a terrible slaying, the only one who might adequately utter the lament.

12

Our Prayers Break on God

Luci Shaw

Our prayers break on God like waves,
and He an endless shore,
and when the seas evaporate
and oceans are no more
and cries are carried on the wind
God hears and answers every sound
As he has done before.

Our troubles eat at God like nails.
He feels the gnaw of pain
on souls and bodies. He never fails
but reassures He'll heal again,
again, again and yet again.

It is good to turn to this beautiful little lyric by Luci Shaw after the concentrated reflection on trauma in Kelly Belmonte's poem. But it is more than just relief, for in one sense Luci's poem might well start where we left off before, with that sense of there being not enough words in the world to say what cannot be said. For this too is a poem about brokenness and pain, but also about how prayers can carry and express that brokenness, and about how God receives those prayers, knows and responds to that pain.

The opening lines are richly ambivalent:

Our prayers break on God like waves,
and He an endless shore,

In one sense we hear the word 'break' speaking to us of our prayers as those of the broken, breaking with those who pray them; and perhaps we think of them as breaking endlessly and futilely on the 'other shore', the unchanged shore of God, as waves break in vain against a cliff. Yet there is another sense in 'break on God', a sense more deeply supported by the rest of the poem: that our prayers break on him in the way that an idea, an insight or a resolve might suddenly break upon us and move us. For this stanza goes on to speak of a God who hears and answers. And God hears and answers just when everything else, for us, has come to an end: when the seas evaporate and oceans are no more. This is more than just an allusion to the verse in Revelation (21.1), that speaks of the end of all things which is also a new beginning: 'Then I saw a new heaven and a new earth; for the first heaven and the first earth had passed away, and the sea was no more.' It is also an evocation of when we ourselves feel dried up and at an ending, and how it is just then, para-doxically, that our prayers break like the waves of the sea, our cries are carried on the wind, and 'God hears and answers every sound'.

But he does more than hear. The second stanza takes us deep into the heart of the gospel, the paradox whereby the sorrow of Jesus is good news to us in our sorrows:

Our troubles eat at God like nails.
He feels the gnaw of pain
on souls and bodies

Here the poetry communicates, in a way that prose never could, that the crucifixion, once for all at a particular moment in time, is also mysteriously the way God himself enters into our pain; or, more profoundly, allows our pain to be hammered into him.

If we have ever felt, as the poet does in the first stanza, that God and his heaven are on some distant shore where the first heave and surge of our grief can only break in tiny wavelets, then the second stanza brings us to the gospel truth that God is close, indeed closer to our pain than we are, that he suffers under the hammer blows of our troubles and our gnawing grief gnaws at him too. But with this difference: our suffering is sometimes only destructive, his is always healing and restorative. Of course, our strength and courage sometimes fail but 'He never fails', and the poem ends with those extraordinary lines, breaking like waves, falling like the hammer blows, not to hurt but to ring out redemption:

He'll heal again,
again, again and yet again.

13

Let Not Your Hearts be Troubled

Malcolm Guite

Let not your heart be troubled: ye believe in God, believe also in me. In my Father's house are many mansions: if it were not so, I would have told you. I go to prepare a place for you. And if I go and prepare a place for you, I will come again, and receive you unto myself; that where I am, there ye may be also. (John 14.1–3, AV)

Always there comes this parting of the ways,
The best is wrested from us, borne away,
No one is with us always, nothing stays,
Night swallows even the most perfect day.
Time makes a tragedy of human love,
We cleave forever to the one we choose
Only to find 'forever' in the grave.
We have just time enough to love and lose.

You know too well this trouble in our hearts,
Your heart is troubled for us, feels it too,
You share with us in time that shears and parts
To draw us out of time and into you.
I go that you might come to where I am
Your word comes home to us and brings us home.

A few years ago I set out to compose a sequence of 50 sonnets on the sayings of Jesus called *Parable and Paradox* in which I voiced, for myself and the reader, not only the joy and awe in hearing his words but also sometimes the struggle, the difficulty, the sense of having to wrestle with a hard saying or wait for particularly mysterious words to open out a little and disclose their depth. I was also mindful, when I wrote that sequence, of the context in which Jesus spoke the sayings, and the context in which we hear them.

When I came to this treasured and beautiful saying in John 14.1–3, it was this second context, the one in which we hear the saying, that leapt out at me. For this is one of the set readings for a funeral service, and of those readings it is the one most often chosen. In their original context these are words of great comfort; they are spoken on the night before Jesus dies, in order to prepare and comfort his disciples, to give them hope. But even then, when they still had Jesus with them in the flesh, the disciples were distracted and confused. In the verses that immediately follow these words of Jesus, Thomas (so-called doubting Thomas – but he should really be called courageous Thomas) says to Jesus, we don't understand, we don't know where you're going, so how can we know the way. In so doing he draws from Jesus that vital truth: 'I am the way, the truth and the life.'

If the disciples found it hard to hear and understand this in its depth even while Jesus was with them, then how must it be for the bereaved and grieving who hear these words, some of them perhaps for the first time, at a funeral? A funeral comes early in the journey of grief, and is such a fraught and demanding day in itself, with all the tasks and troubles in its preparation, that I wonder how much we can give to or draw from these words when we hear them then.

This is why in my sonnet I devote the whole of the first part (the octet) to what the bereaved person at the funeral might be feeling in their depths even as these words roll over them and vanish into the air, for unless that is acknowledged first, the words themselves will mean nothing. This first part of the sonnet confesses the inevitability of loss for all of us: 'Always there comes this parting of the ways'.

That truth is woven even into the marriage service, when we promise 'to love and to cherish till death us do part', and that is part of what loving and cherishing mean – to know and for the loved one's sake to embrace the eventual pain of loss. We could keep ourselves secure from grief by loving no one, but to love someone – anyone – is to say, 'I am prepared to be vulnerable for your sake.' In that sense our grief, when it comes, is chosen, and nobly chosen. It is borne for the sake and in the honour of the belovèd whom we mourn, but that doesn't make it any easier to bear.

And when that parting comes it is always too soon, always and without exception tragic, for when we love someone that love kindles a sense of the eternal in us; we naturally reach for the word 'forever', 'only to find "forever" in the grave'.

It is only with this understanding that something that should remain whole has been broken that we can hear the words of one who has entered into that breach and brokenness for us.

So it is only after the *volta* in my sonnet, in the sestet, that I turn to Jesus, and change from the 'we' of our shared human mortality to address Jesus himself, who is both fully human like us and also fully God. I address him familiarly, but also in awe as 'you':

You know too well this trouble in our hearts,
Your heart is troubled for us, feels it too,
You share with us in time that shears and parts
To draw us out of time and into you.

The God I speak to already knows and shares my suffering. I don't have to hide it from him. If he says, 'Let not your hearts be troubled', it is not because he doesn't understand how troubled our hearts actually are, or doesn't feel that trouble too. On the contrary, it is because he feels and knows it only too well that he wants to heal it for us. It is not his will that death should do this to us or that our hearts should always be troubled, for he has come not only to share the trouble but to deal with it, to mend the break and heal the wound that time, in all its shearing and parting, has made. He has prepared a place for us beyond the time, and that place is his own heart, the very heart of love in heaven. He will draw us out of time and into himself, and so he says these words to us now, in the midst of our pain, that we may still have hope. In the final couplet I hear Jesus speak again, calling me to be where he is, knowing that the belovèd for whom I mourn is also there with Jesus. And knowing that, I can end my sonnet as I hope to end my days, with homecoming.

PART 3

Loving Lament

The bitter-sweet experience of loving through sorrow

Introduction

In Part 2 our poetry was expressing in various ways the immediate shock of loss, when the spirit seems numb and frozen and the mind can scarcely find words; but, as some of the poems suggest, we do eventually move beyond that stage. Tears release memory and memory releases tears: Elizabeth Barrett Browning's frozen statue is able to weep and move again. After the first shock we move into a bitter-sweet country in which both love and lament are intertwined, seeming to spring from the same root and flourish on the same stem. Sometimes the lament is so real, the pain so overpowering, and both clearly springing from our having loved and lost, that we are tempted for a moment to wish that we have never loved at all, since love leaves us so vulnerable. Once again, the searing honesty of Tennyson's *In Memoriam* can come to our aid. When we last visited this poem he gave us in his first shock of grief the images of the frozen lake, the foundering ship and the delirious man, but as we read on from that early section, the lake unfreezes, the ship steadies a little and the man finds his feet and begins to remember joy, even when that memory brings pain. Tennyson faces squarely the fact that it is love itself that exposes him to pain and is at the root of his lament. As he does so *In Memoriam* rises to a climax in the great Section XXVII which concludes with perhaps the most famous lines of the poem:

I envy not in any moods
The captive void of noble rage,
The linnet born within the cage,
That never knew the summer woods:

I envy not the beast that takes
His license in the field of time,
Unfetter'd by the sense of crime,
To whom a conscience never wakes;

Nor, what may count itself as blest,
The heart that never plighted troth
But stagnates in the weeds of sloth;
Nor any want-begotten rest.

I hold it true, whate'er befall;
I feel it, when I sorrow most;
'Tis better to have loved and lost
Than never to have loved at all.

In the narrative arc of the poem this section comes just before
the first Christmas after Hallam's death, the first of the anni-
versaries that Tennyson will have to face alone. It represents a
kind of gathering of courage and resolve to face those hard days.
When the memory of joy is so painful, can we wish that we had
never experienced that joy? In a series of beautiful images and
emblems Tennyson answers with a resounding 'no'. He starts
by rejecting the shrunken world of diminished expectations and
contented captivity. 'The captive void of noble rage' may be an
echo of Thomas Gray's famous 'Elegy in a Country Churchyard',
lamenting how people kept in poverty lost the anger that should
have resisted their conditions:

Chill Penury repress'd their noble rage
And froze the genial current of the soul.

Tennyson will not let grief freeze the genial current in himself,
or in us. If grief is sometimes like a cage, we must remember
that we were neither born in it nor born for it. In the second
stanza, Tennyson realises that to shrink from the pain of grief
and wish we had never loved is to wish away what makes us
most fully human, and that includes our gifts of moral choice

and conscience. When conscience stops us from doing just as we like, we might envy the animals who seem to lack it, but to do so would be to wish ourselves less human. And so, after these glimpses of the bird in the cage and beast in the field, Tennyson turns in the third stanza to our own humanity. To plight our troth, gladly to give ourselves away in love and not to guard the heart but to open it: this is what makes us human, however much in our grief we might look at the un-plighted heart, keeping itself to itself, as somehow blessed. It is not blessing, says Tennyson, but stagnation:

> Nor, what may count itself as blest,
> The heart that never plighted troth
> But stagnates in the weeds of sloth;

This verse and indeed this section of Tennyson's poem is, I think, the source and seed for C. S. Lewis' often quoted words in *The Four Loves*:

> To love at all is to be vulnerable. Love anything and your heart will be wrung and possibly broken. If you want to make sure of keeping it intact you must give it to no one, not even an animal. Wrap it carefully round with hobbies and little luxuries; avoid all entanglements. Lock it up safe in the casket or coffin of your selfishness. But in that casket, safe, dark, motionless, airless, it will change. It will not be broken; it will become unbreakable, impenetrable, irredeemable. To love is to be vulnerable.

Then in the final stanza of this section, Tennyson's poetry rises to the simple but unforgettable expression of a truth that is felt instinctively, and learned slowly through time:

> I hold it true, whate'er befall;
> I feel it, when I sorrow most;
> 'Tis better to have loved and lost
> Than never to have loved at all.

Once we have accepted this, then we can open up; we can look around us and move forward through the bitter-sweet country of loving lament. We will not be afraid that our crying and lamentation might injure our love or cast a shadow on the belovèd, for they are in their own way expressions of that love and a tribute to its object. Nor will we be afraid that remembering vividly and speaking often and lovingly of the person we have lost, perhaps with unexpected laughter and little stabs of joy, in any way trivialises or diminishes our proper grief. We won't have to call a funeral 'a celebration' with a forced smile, for we will know that to lament for someone is itself to celebrate what you loved in them. The poems in this part will help, I hope, in their different ways to express this double truth of love and lamentation.

14

The Grieving Ground

Adrian Rice

Reaching the why and wherefore of the racket –
A blackbird lying by the garden gate
And her mate protesting from branch to branch –
I sensed something, turned and glanced
And caught him staring from his kitchen window.
I didn't mouth a word or make a sign,
But I knew he knew what was wrong.
He struggled round, put on a scary show,
But failed to stop the sorrow song
Or force the living from the grieving ground.
I shyly watched him shoo at grief,
Remembering the loss of his own wife,
And realized Death, the homeless thief,
Had broken in, squatted and wouldn't leave.

This poem comes from a sequence 'The Moongate Sonnets', published in *The Clock Flower* in 2013 by Adrian Rice, an Ulster poet now living in North Carolina. The sonnet sequence is dedicated to an elderly neighbour, Billy Montgomery, an 'honest Ulsterman', and in paying him just and due attention Rice gives us his take not only on a whole locale and its people but on the way the universal is best expressed through the particular. The poet Dante Gabriel Rossetti, writing in a sonnet about the sonnet as a poetic form, famously said that 'a sonnet is a moment's monument'. Good sonnets, like this one, can certainly capture a particular moment and everything that wider moment means, while the sequence as a whole is a monument in the sense of being a memorial to the dead, to Billy Montgomery. Even as Rice tells us something about Billy's grief for his wife, he also expresses his own; and he tells us something about our grief too. The poem begins boldly, 'Reaching the why and wherefore of the racket', and does indeed explain the source of 'the racket' that has attracted the attention of both Billy and the poet: the protesting lament of a blackbird at the death of its mate. But beyond that racket the poem can only gesture towards the deeper whys and wherefores of our own lamentation.

> I sensed something, turned and glanced
> And caught him staring from his kitchen window.

That image of the two men distanced by the glass pane and the length of the garden, one suddenly sensing the other's grief, with the griever feeling almost that he has been caught in a moment of weakness from which the poet shies away, expresses so much of the reserve inherent in the culture of Ulster, and perhaps in most men of that generation. Nevertheless, the dead bird, the 'blackbird lying by the garden gate', and the loud grief of its mate deftly express for these two reticent men both Billy's displaced grief for his wife and later the poet's grief for Billy.

For all 'the racket' that the bird makes, there is a classic northern reticence, a deference and understatement between the two men:

> I didn't mouth a word or make a sign,
> But I knew he knew what was wrong.

But even their reticence and reserve cannot 'stop the sorrow song' of their own grief any more than they can scare away the grieving bird. In the end, the poem refuses to 'force the living from the grieving ground', however shy or reticent, that grief needs to be in public.

I shyly watched him shoo at grief,
Remembering the loss of his own wife,
And realized Death, the homeless thief,
Had broken in, squatted, and wouldn't leave.

There is so much going on in this vivid, understated poem, from
the way the bird's grief carries ours to the way the rhymes in
the final four lines play slantwise off one another and refuse
the fullness of closure, a refusal that is itself the subject of the
poem; 'leave' tries but fails to rhyme with 'thief'. While many of
the sonnets in Rice's sequence witness to the incompleteness of
the momentary and the way moments themselves are broken by
grief and death, the whole sequence still carries the sense of the
finished and well-wrought monument. This is particularly so in
the final poem, 'The Double Crown', to which we will turn in
our penultimate part, 'Receiving'.

15

Bitter-Sweet

George Herbert

Ah, my dear angry Lord,
Since Thou dost love, yet strike;
Cast down, yet help afford;
Sure I will do the like.

I will complain, yet praise;
I will bewail, approve:
And all my sour-sweet days
I will lament, and love.

I spoke in the introduction to this part of our need to move
forward through the bitter-sweet country of loving lament. So it
is appropriate to reflect on Herbert's poem 'Bitter-Sweet', which
his recent biographer John Drury has called 'one of his con-
summately crafted miniatures'. It is a brief poem but every line,
indeed every word, is telling, and what they tell of most deeply
is the importance of holding our contrary experiences together,
of not simplifying but rather gathering insight and energy from
the creative tensions in which our lives are held. Like its title, the
whole poem holds and yokes together apparent contradictions
and leaves the reader to feel the different pulses of exchange and
reciprocity like the force fields of a magnet. So in the opening
line, 'Ah, my dear angry Lord', although Herbert is complaining
to God, and he feels as though God is angry with him, yet this

Lord is still his own and his belovèd. Their steadfast covenant love is a frame well able to contain these energies of contradiction, and Herbert's Lord, is still addressed with that quiet intimacy, so typical of Herbert, as 'my dear'.

The rest of this verse deepens the sense of contrariety and locates it in God's own actions and not simply Herbert's response: 'Thou dost love, yet strike; cast down, yet help afford'. We are all happy to say that God loves and helps us, but can we say that he strikes us and casts us down? Whatever the final theological truth, we can certainly say that that is what it sometimes feels like. It is precisely because we love and trust God and sense that we, and all things, are in his hands that when we experience the harsh blows that life sometimes deals us we cannot help turning to God in our pain, as though he, our belovèd, has struck the blow. That is how the psalmists in the Old Testament felt and wrote, and indeed this poem of Herbert's is full of echoes of the Psalter that he loved and prayed every day. For the Psalter contains all the contradictions in this poem and the strange polarity of its different responses; sometimes they are contained in a single psalm, as they are in this single poem. One thinks of the opening of Psalm 38:

O Lord, do not rebuke me in your anger,
or discipline me in your wrath.
For your arrows have sunk into me,
and your hand has come down upon me.

And yet that same psalm, even as it feels what seems to be the Lord's rebuke, still speaks to that Lord with a lover-like intimacy:

O Lord, all my longing is known to you;
my sighing is not hidden from you.
My heart throbs, my strength fails me;

For all its agony, the psalm never lets God go, and calls God in its final verse, 'O Lord, my salvation'.

In the last line of Herbert's first verse comes a sudden and daring turn: 'Sure I will do the like'. It is as though Herbert is saying to God, if you can do this to me, then it must be all right for me to do the same to you! Considering that this seems to be a poem, of complaint and agony, there is a strange confidence in this – a sense that he can trust the underlying foundation of his relationship with God enough to let it have its ups and downs. And the great fruit of this, for Herbert and for us, is that it allows total honesty, we no longer have to filter our feelings and keep them back from God. If we are angry (and all the bereaved are understandably angry) then we can be openly angry with God: 'I will complain'! If we have nothing to offer but tears and sorrow, then we can offer those to God: 'I will bewail', 'I will lament'. But then, paradoxically, we find, with the psalmist and with Herbert, that such frank expression of pain and hurt does not break the relationship but actually deepens its intimacy; it honestly clears the air and opens the heart.

And so, just as the psalms often turn on the words 'yet' or 'nevertheless', and move from lament to praise, so Herbert contracts those great movements into a single line: 'I will complain, *yet* praise'. Then, more concentratedly, comes the juxtaposition of two words, 'bewail, approve', and then finally he opens it out into a definitively conclusive statement, an approach that is 'both/and' rather than 'either/or': 'I will lament, *and* love'. So throughout this poem there is balance and reciprocity between lamentation and love, and complete honesty about our bittersweet experience of life. But it is equally important to say that love has the last word, for it is no accident that this poem ends literally with 'love'. Here, Herbert perhaps intuits for us some relief for when we feel in our grief that God himself is hurting us. Surely that cannot be, for he is Love; our only way forward in this impasse is to say that if the God who is love is involved in our pains, then whatever else is happening he is feeling our grief in us, with us and through us, not apart from us.

16

A sequence from *Adonais*

Percy Bysshe Shelley

XVIII

Ah, woe is me! Winter is come and gone,
But grief returns with the revolving year;
The airs and streams renew their joyous tone;
The ants, the bees, the swallows reappear;
Fresh leaves and flowers deck the dead Seasons' bier;
The amorous birds now pair in every brake,
And build their mossy homes in field and brere;
And the green lizard, and the golden snake,
Like unimprison'd flames, out of their trance awake.

XIX

Through wood and stream and field and hill and Ocean
A quickening life from the Earth's heart has burst
As it has ever done, with change and motion,
From the great morning of the world when first
God dawn'd on Chaos; in its stream immers'd,
The lamps of Heaven flash with a softer light;
All baser things pant with life's sacred thirst;
Diffuse themselves; and spend in love's delight,
The beauty and the joy of their renewed might.

XX

The leprous corpse, touch'd by this spirit tender,
Exhales itself in flowers of gentle breath;
Like incarnations of the stars, when splendour
Is chang'd to fragrance, they illumine death
And mock the merry worm that wakes beneath;
Nought we know, dies. Shall that alone which knows
Be as a sword consum'd before the sheath
By sightless lightning? – the intense atom glows
A moment, then is quench'd in a most cold repose.

XXI

Alas! that all we lov'd of him should be,
But for our grief, as if it had not been,
And grief itself be mortal! Woe is me!
Whence are we, and why are we? of what scene
The actors or spectators? Great and mean
Meet mass'd in death, who lends what life must borrow.
As long as skies are blue, and fields are green,
Evening must usher night, night urge the morrow,
Month follow month with woe, and year wake year to sorrow.

These verses are from Shelley's beautiful pastoral elegy lamenting the untimely death of John Keats. The two poets had met a few years earlier in Hampstead and Shelley was one of the few at that time who recognised and nurtured Keats' poetic gift. Shelley felt a deep kinship with him; they exchanged letters, and he invited Keats to stay with him in Pisa to recover his health. Indeed Shelley, always generous in his judgement, perhaps because he was condemned as harshly by his own contemporaries as Keats had been, wrote: 'I am aware indeed that I am nourishing a rival who will far surpass me and this is an additional motive & will be an added pleasure.' This elegy has added poignancy as Shelley himself died young, not long after he wrote it, something he seemed to foresee at the end of the work; when his body was recovered from the waters in which he drowned there was a copy of Keats' poems in his jacket pocket.

But though the elegy is very personal and particular in another sense it is universal. Generation after generation of readers have turned to it to find voice for their feelings, most famously in recent times when Mick Jagger read verses from this poem to 300,000 people at a memorial concert in Hyde Park after the death of Brian Jones.

One way in which the particular becomes universal here is in Shelley's choice of the classical pastoral elegy as his means of expression. The ancient world has bequeathed to us a beautiful form of lament in both Greek and Latin poetry in which personal grief is transposed into a beautiful pastoral setting: a world of nymphs and shepherds in which the lost belovèd is lamented in an evocation of the natural world. In the pastoral elegy the groves, fields and flowers all in some way reflect or comment on our grief. Milton had introduced this mode of writing into English in his pastoral elegy 'Lycidas', lamenting the death of fellow poet Edward King, and now Shelley takes up the same strain, aware that Keats too had used this pastoral mode of poetry in his long poem *Endymion*.

This is the first of two extracts from *Adonais* that we will read in this anthology. Shelley gives us the almost unbearable contrast between the renewal of all things in spring (Keats died in April and Shelley began his poem in May) and the sense of loss and all that is left unrenewed and wintry in the heart of the mourner.

So in the first stanza of this extract are a series of contrasting phrases; the poet's tone is one of lament – 'Ah, woe is me' – yet he also hears and responds to the joyous tone of the season: 'grief returns' and yet the 'streams renew'. Then in a reimagining of the funeral flowers for a friend he sees that the 'Fresh leaves and flowers' of spring are also a kind of funeral tribute but they 'deck the dead Seasons' bier'. For them it is winter that has died, not a belovèd friend whose life and poetry were so full of the promise of spring. And after that line the poetry suddenly leaps up, even in the midst of its lament, with a beautiful celebration of a spring that in itself knows no grief:

The amorous birds now pair in every brake,
And build their mossy homes in field and brere;
And the green lizard, and the golden snake,
Like unimprison'd flames, out of their trance awake

There is a wonderful sense of life returning in the 'unimprison'd flames', waking from a trance, and surely those images must carry with them some hint, some rumour, of resurrection.

The next stanza develops that further, with its resonant imagery of beginnings and renewals, of life bursting from 'Earth's heart', the sense that every spring renews, 'the great morning of the world'. It is the moment of creation in which Shelley imagines God as a light dawning on chaos, and the divine light itself softening and infusing his new creation with delight and joy. Shelley described himself as an atheist – indeed, it was for his atheism that he was expelled from his college, and the reason he was deprived of custody of his children – but none of his great poems are in any modern sense 'atheist'. They are suffused with a sense of the divine, a celebration of light in darkness; his 'Ode to the West Wind', perhaps his most famous poem after *Adonais*, reads to anyone versed in scripture like an invocation of the Holy Spirit. Shelley chose the label 'atheist' because he was morally outraged by the way institutional Christianity had become a force for oppression and cruelty in the world, but he was never, as the term sometimes now implies, a reductive materialist. He delighted in the beauty of the world but also saw it as shot through with a radiance from beyond itself. For Shelley the whole cosmos was an immense stained-glass window through which the divine light was continually pouring. Indeed, later in this poem he describes all life as 'a dome of many-coloured glass' that 'stains the white radiance of eternity'.

However, the intense awareness of beauty and renewal in the world of nature so memorably expressed in this second stanza does not make grief any less real, but rather brings it into greater contrast and focus.

So in stanza XX Shelley brings in suddenly, without evasion or euphemism, the fearful and difficult image of the 'leprous corpse', and shows how that too is taken up in the great renewals and transformations of spring:

> The leprous corpse, touch'd by this spirit tender,
> Exhales itself in flowers of gentle breath;
> Like incarnations of the stars, when splendour
> Is chang'd to fragrance, they illumine death

Even the lost body is changed by spring to beauty, and there is a wonderful metaphor here of change and modulation, of one kind of being transposed into another, which in itself may whisper hope to our grief. The new blossom and patterning of flowers on the grass are seen as being like 'incarnations of the stars', so the splendour of light in the pattern of white stars flowering in heaven is now 'chang'd to fragrance' in the flowers over the grave, and just as the stars illumine the darkness of night, so these new flowers 'illumine death'. And there is more. The flowers themselves are exhaled, they are breathed into being by a 'spirit tender'. The creation imagery is unmistakable, and in the biblical narrative the stars are also breathed into being, called forth by the word and by the breath of God, the 'Spirit' moving on the face of the deep. It is the very contrast between this breathing and renewal in spring and the sense of the breath of human spiritual life having gone from the 'leprous corpse' that poignantly poses to us a sharp question. And Shelley goes on to ask that question with courage and honesty:

> Nought we know, dies. Shall that alone which knows
> Be as a sword consum'd before the sheath
> By sightless lightning?

How can it be, amid all this quickening and beautiful renewal of the physical, that the spiritual should die? The spiritual is 'that alone which knows', for neither the flowers nor the stars know their own beauty. But Keats and Shelley have seen and celebrated the flowers and the stars and *know* their beauty. Surely, Shelley is saying, that power in us to know and love nature and to see and celebrate the renewal of life must also itself be renewed. He notices our moments of wakening in this life and says, look, even in this life we have scarcely drawn the sword of our spirit from the sheath of the body: shall the spirit be consumed and die in that sheath before it has the chance to flash out and shine in all its glory? Of course, he knows that at the physical level something has come and gone:

> the intense atom glows
> A moment, then is quench'd in a most cold repose.

But can that be all? Shelley faces that possibility, and even in the midst of beauty he laments:

> Alas! that all we lov'd of him should be,
> But for our grief, as if it had not been,
> And grief itself be mortal! Woe is me!

But in the midst of lamentation the questions keep coming:

> Whence are we, and why are we? of what scene
> The actors or spectators?

This is not atheism, but rather agnosticism at its best. Shelley is feeling the contradictions, pressing the questions, restlessly questing for answers; as we shall see in Part 6 of this anthology, he does indeed receive and express an answer to these universal questions. But even as he waits, he continues to give voice to the experience of countless others on their long journey through grief, constant to their loving lament through all the changing seasons:

> As long as skies are blue, and fields are green,
> Evening must usher night, night urge the morrow,
> Month follow month with woe, and year wake year to
>   sorrow.

17

The Voice

Thomas Hardy

Woman much missed, how you call to me, call to me,
Saying that now you are not as you were
When you had changed from the one who was all to me,
But as at first, when our day was fair.

Can it be you that I hear? Let me view you, then,
Standing as when I drew near to the town
Where you would wait for me: yes, as I knew you then,
Even to the original air-blue gown!

Or is it only the breeze, in its listlessness
Travelling across the wet mead to me here,
You being ever dissolved to wan wistlessness,
Heard no more again far or near?

Thus I; faltering forward,
Leaves around me falling,
Wind oozing thin through the thorn from norward,
And the woman calling.

With this poem we return to Thomas Hardy's moving sequence
of poems of 1912–13, written as a response to the death of his
wife Emma, which we first encountered in 'The Going' in Part 1
of this book. 'The Voice' comes later in the sequence, after the

first shock and loss recorded in the earlier poem. In this poem we have a sense not so much of going as of returning, of Hardy's deep memories of Emma, awakened by grief, calling out to him over and over. He had perhaps anticipated that this would happen in the third verse of 'The Going':

Why do you make me leave the house
And think for a breath it is you I see
At the end of the alley of bending boughs?

Like that poem, 'The Voice' is aware, as it were, of a double gap between the poet and his belovèd: the gap between the living and the departed and that between Emma as she had been when Hardy first knew and loved her and the woman she became later when they had both changed and drifted apart. But now her voice calls, as intensely as ever, across both gaps; perhaps it is the haunting repetition of the words 'call to me, call to me', that suggests both meanings. The whole of the poem yearns across that gap, listens intently for that voice, accepts the terrible irony that having let that first love between them fade and die, having ceased to see in her the woman he had fallen in love with, Hardy has come at last to hear her calling 'as at first, when our day was fair'; but now it is too late.

But that repetition of 'call to me, call to me' in the opening line does more than just evoke the double gulf across which Emma calls; it also establishes a distinct rhythm that is an essential part of the poem's meaning.

Much of the poetry in this book, indeed most classic English poetry, is written in iambic pentameter. An iamb is a unit of rhythm that goes from unstressed to stressed: 'ta-*tum*'. There are usually five of these iambs to a line, making for a quiet pulse to the poem very like the beating of the heart. But many other metres and rhythms are possible, and for this poem Hardy uses the rarer dactyl. This has a strong first beat followed by two unstressed ones: '*tum*-ta-ta'. You can hear three perfect dactyls in the line from the nursery rhyme: 'All the king's horses and all the king's men'. For the first three verses of this poem Hardy deploys this dactylic meter beautifully, with four dactyls to each line. If you read these verses aloud you cannot help hearing a kind of haunting waltz behind the words, '*tum*-ta-ta' being also the rhythm of the dance. The effect in this poem is to suggest that as the bereft widower addresses the soul of his lost wife and seems to hear her 'call to me, call to me', we hear, from the depths of time, the waltz music to which they danced in their youth. We are caught up for a moment as he whirls her around in her 'air-blue gown'. But the music is only a memory borne on the listless breeze. Even as we hear it, the music is 'dissolved to wan wistlessness' and in the final verse the metre changes. The music is gone for ever, the rhythm falters even as we come to the word 'faltering', which is itself the last dactyl in the poem. The rhythm of 'Leaves around me falling, Wind oozing thin' is quite different, uncertain, subdued, as you will hear if you say the poem out loud.

Hardy's strange dance of love and lament peters out, his courage falters along with the poem itself, and Hardy brushes aside the illusions of memory and confesses that as he lives on without Emma, 'faltering forward', coming to the autumn of his years, all seems bleak and thin. And yet it is the voice of the belovèd – loved and lamented, the woman 'much missed', the voice of the title and the opening lines – that is the last thing we hear. Hardy strains through his pain to catch the echo of that lost music: 'the woman calling'.

18

On My First Son

Ben Jonson

Farewell, thou child of my right hand, and joy;
My sin was too much hope of thee, lov'd boy.
Seven years tho' wert lent to me, and I thee pay,
Exacted by thy fate, on the just day.
O, could I lose all father now! For why
Will man lament the state he should envy?
To have so soon 'scap'd world's and flesh's rage,
And if no other misery, yet age?
Rest in soft peace, and, ask'd, say here doth lie
Ben Jonson his best piece of poetry.
For whose sake henceforth all his vows be such,
As what he loves may never like too much.

Ben Jonson (1572–1637) was Shakespeare's friend and younger
contemporary. Like Constance in Shakespeare's *King John*,
a passage we looked at in Part 2, Jonson here confronts the
appalling experience of the death of a child, but his approach is
different from Shakespeare's. Shakespeare may well have been
expressing his own grief at the loss of his son Hamnet, through
the speeches he gives to Constance. But because he was speaking
through a character in a drama and not directly in his own voice,
Shakespeare could, paradoxically, say more: he could allow
Constance in the play to give a longer, stronger, wilder expres-
sion of grief than he dared to allow himself in life, both because

of the constraints of social convention and also, perhaps, for fear of complete breakdown.

Here, by contrast, Jonson speaks directly and personally, and while the poem exposes the depth of his grief and the tenderness of his feelings, it also has about it a strong element of control, dignity and restraint, which Jonson almost certainly felt he owed to those around him and needed for himself.

Jonson's eldest son, also named Benjamin Jonson, died in 1603 at the age of seven having contracted bubonic plague. Jonson probably composed this poem shortly after his son's death but did not publish it until 1616, when he included it in a collection of epigraphs. Most of the other epigraphs are satiric, witty, occasionally cynical; not so this one, which stands out from the rest of the collection, as having, for all its formal grace and classic structure, such a personal and vulnerable tone. Like so many bereaved parents, Jonson feels the need to address his child directly, rather than just write about him, and so the poem begins with the word that most needs to be said by the bereaved, but is sometimes hardest to say: 'Farewell'. But that first line tells us so much more. 'Farewell, thou child of my right hand, and joy'. Jonson is delicately alluding to the meaning of his son's name, and indeed to the poignant biblical story out of which Benjamin was named. He is thinking of Genesis 35.16–18:

> Then they journeyed from Bethel; and when they were still some distance from Ephrath, Rachel was in childbirth, and she had a difficult labour. When she was in her difficult labour, the midwife said to her, 'Do not be afraid; for now you will have another son.' As her soul was departing (for she died), she named him Ben-oni; but his father called him Benjamin.

So he is thinking of Jacob and Rachel on their strange journey and of Rachel in her difficult labour. Jonson also knew something of the loss of a parent at birth; his father died a month before he was born, leaving Jonson and his mother struggling. Jonson, who made so much of his life later, began on a lowly rung as an apprentice bricklayer, supplementing his widowed mother's meagre income. But the important thing for this poem is the naming: the name that Rachel chose in her agony was Ben-oni, which means 'son of my sorrows', but the name that Jacob chose, in the midst of grief for his wife but for joy at the survival of his son, was Benjamin, which means 'son of my right hand', a phrase that also came to mean 'fortune' or 'joy'. This key family story in Genesis goes on, as Ben Jonson knew only too well, to tell the tale of how Jacob, having lost Joseph, also feared that he had lost this belovèd last son, little Benjamin. So for a moment Jonson, though himself also called Benjamin, becomes father Jacob in both his joy and his sorrow. The poem goes on to explore the paradoxes of that joy and sorrow, being addressed, even after death, in the present tense to the child – alive to God, though absent from his father. Benjamin is still for Jonson, in his grief, his 'child', his 'joy', his 'lov'd boy'.

Early in the poem, Jonson rebukes himself for having placed too much hope on things turning out well in this world, invested too much not in the love itself but in a father's hopes and ambitions for his child: 'My sin was too much hope of thee, lov'd boy.' Then he goes on to echo the words of Job (that other bereaved father) about the Lord giving and the Lord taking away, and sees that in some sense his child had only been *lent* to him for a time. Although there is desperation in the line 'Seven years tho' wert lent to me, and I thee pay', there is also confidence, for to whom can he pay his little Benjamin but to God? So, however hard it is to say 'I thee pay', it is also saying that his 'lov'd boy' is safe with his other Father in heaven. It must have taken both effort and courage to write this poem and also, paradoxically, to call the day of Benjamin's death, one that must have felt disastrous, 'the just day'. Then, as though emotionally exhausted by that very effort, Jonson seems to give in to the temptation that we saw Tennyson fighting in the introduction to this part, and writes: 'O, could I lose all father now.'

At one level, he is certainly saying that his feelings as a father are so painful that he wishes he could relinquish them, but at another level he is preparing himself for what comes next in the poem: the deeper truth, which Jonson's strong Christian faith affirms, that a father's tragic loss has been redeemed in Christ, for Benjamin has escaped the 'world's and flesh's rage'. The 'flesh's rage' surely alludes to the terrible pains endured by a child suffering from the plague. Then in lines 9 and 10 Jonson comes to the heart of the poem and its most beautiful and enduring passage: a blessing and the poet's reimagining of his own child as poetry:

> Rest in soft peace, and, ask'd, say here doth lie
> Ben Jonson his best piece of poetry.

The phrase 'Ben Jonson his best' is an early form of the possessive; nowadays we would say 'Ben Jonson's best'. There is something stately in Jonson's use of this older form. Poets have often thought of their poems as children, with the sense of giving birth to them, sending them out into the world and hoping they will make friends and mean as much to other people as they mean to the author. But here Jonson turns that around and sees his child as incomparably better than all his poetry, as the best of his 'works'.

In the final couplet of the poem Jonson tries to move forward and to see what he can learn from this bitter experience:

> For whose sake henceforth all his vows be such,
> As what he loves may never like too much.

How can he now, for his son's sake, learn how to love without always needing to hold on and to possess? He does this by making a distinction between 'love' and 'like' which can seem puzzling to the modern reader. I don't think Jonson is saying that we shouldn't *like* those we *love* in the modern sense of 'like'; rather he is saying that all those we love must be loved freely for their own sake. We should not desire to possess them and we must ultimately be willing to let them go to their own bliss rather than clinging to them simply to please our own private 'liking'.

For all its outward appearance of classical finality, like a carved epitaph, one has a sense that this poem is struggling

unsuccessfully to contain an unresolved conflict. Jonson strug-
gled on through his own bereavement and did indeed write much
great poetry – though never, as he says here, as great as the son
he lost. In an addendum to this story, later in his life Jonson had
many young followers among the rising generation of poets and
they used to call themselves 'the tribe of Ben', alluding to the
Genesis passage, but sometimes, more intimately and perhaps
with reference to Jonson's own loss, they called themselves 'the
sons of Ben'.

19

Onlookers

Luci Shaw

Behind our shield of health, each
of us must sense another's anguish
second-hand; we are agnostic
in the face of dying. So Joseph
felt, observer of the push
and splash of birth, and even Mary,
mourner, under the cross's arm.
Only their son, and God's,
in bearing all our griefs
felt them first-hand, climbing
himself our rugged hill of pain.
His nerves, enfleshed, carried
the messages of nails, the tomb's
chill. His ever-open wounds
still blazon back to us the penalty
we never bore, and heaven
gleams for us more real,
crossed with that human blood.

Throughout this book we have been, in one sense, onlookers on
the grief of others. The poetry has enabled us to come close. It
has kindled our imagination, peeled away some of the layers of
self-protective distance and indifference, exposed us to truths we
sometimes shun; at its best it has summoned our own feelings of

loss so that a shared experience can bring us closer to others. But there is only so much that poetry, even great poetry, can do, and Luci Shaw's strong poem 'Onlookers' confronts that fact; it also offers us a way to move beyond it.

She starts with the experience of all those who visit the sick yet are themselves in good health – the sense of not really knowing what the other person is going through, however much we want to empathise:

Behind our shield of health, each
of us must sense another's anguish
second-hand;

And if that is true of visiting the sick, how much more is it the case in our attempts to reach and comfort the dying:

we are agnostic
in the face of dying.

We are agnostic in the literal sense that we simply do not know what dying is like, and that sense of a gulf or disjunction between our own experience and that of even our nearest and dearest is well expressed by the way the word 'agnostic' is left cut off from the rest of its sentence at the end of a line. We are not even on the same line as the dying, and yet we long to be; our love wants more than anything to bridge the gap.

But if the opening lines of this poem identify all of us as helpless onlookers then at least we are not alone. Luci Shaw immediately puts us in the good company of Mary and Joseph, onlookers of one another's pain and the pain of their son.

She shows us Joseph, looking on at Mary's pain in childbirth, loving her through it, yet knowing that he can neither share nor relieve it. And then we flash forward to Mary herself, looking on at the suffering of her son, the life and joy she bore through pain, a mourner now, 'under the cross's arm'. There is something poignant about the word 'arm' here, applied to an inanimate and unfeeling object, the wooden cross, when we know that it is the

warm and tender arm of Jesus stretched out in love for us that
bears the pain, while Mary's arms that once cradled him now
stand empty beneath the arm of the cross.

And then comes the great turn of the poem, beginning with
the word 'Only'. We see that God himself does for us what we
cannot do for ourselves: bridging that unbearable gap, and really
feeling and bearing another's grief as he bears ours:

> Only their son, and God's,
> in bearing all our griefs
> felt them first-hand, climbing
> himself our rugged hill of pain.

This is no abstract or mythological encounter, no pain-bearing
only in the realm of story and idea. Luci Shaw is a poet of the
incarnation, of the word made flesh:

> His nerves, enfleshed, carried
> the messages of nails, the tomb's
> chill.

In some ways these lines take us back to her poem in Part 2
of this anthology, 'Our Prayers Break on God', and her words,
'Our troubles eat at God like nails'. Here she locates that com-
passion in the Passion itself.

But was it only for then, only for that Good Friday? Is that
episode in which God felt our pain from the inside all over now?
This poem says no! The Passion is not so much ended as trans-
figured:

> His ever-open wounds
> still blazon back to us the penalty
> we never bore, and heaven
> gleams for us more real,
> crossed with that human blood.

These lines, faithfully witnessing to the Gospel accounts that Jesus still bore his wounds in the resurrection and that they were a source of renewed faith and healing for the disciples, also echo perhaps the hymn that speaks of 'Those wounds yet visible above in beauty glorified'. In her final lines Luci Shaw does something beautiful with the word 'crossed'. First there is the sense of the reality of heaven itself, not distant and abstract but 'more real' because it is 'crossed' with human blood, because the Lord of heaven had a heart that beat like ours. And there is also the sense of crossing from one side to another, of joining what has been separated. We realise that this word 'crossed' is the very word we longed for when in the opening lines we found it impossible to cross the divide between ourselves and another's grief. And finally there is, of course, running just beneath both these senses of 'crossed', the cross itself, for it is by the cross that heaven is crossed with earth and the dividing lines that once isolated us in our grief are crossed by the One who has come in his love to bear our grief with us.

PART 4

Remembrance of Things Past

Everything reminds us, painfully or poignantly of the belovèd

Introduction

As we pass some of these staging posts in the journey of grief, our memory comes and goes, renews itself, is suddenly triggered in fresh ways. That renewal of memory becomes, as we said in the Introduction, both a delight and a despair. But just as we must both love and lament, so too we must follow Ophelia's bidding: 'love, remember'. All the poems in this part meditate in some way on these sudden stabs of memory, on the way memory is embedded in time and also lifts us out of time. Many things can trigger memory, and those triggers are both expected and unexpected. We expect, and perhaps dread, the days that are already set aside for remembrance: wedding anniversaries, birthdays, the first anniversary of a loss. It may sometimes feel that these are simply days to be 'got through', but they may also have something to teach us. To help with introducing this particular stage in our journey let us dip once more into *In Memoriam*, Tennyson's grief journal, and see how in Section XCIX he approaches that most difficult of days, the anniversary of his loss:

Risest thou thus, dim dawn, again,
So loud with voices of the birds,
So thick with lowings of the herds,
Day, when I lost the flower of men;

Who tremblest thro' thy darkling red
On yon swoll'n brook that bubbles fast
By meadows breathing of the past,
And woodlands holy to the dead;

Who murmurest in the foliaged eaves
A song that slights the coming care,
And Autumn laying here and there
A fiery finger on the leaves;

Who wakenest with thy balmy breath
To myriads on the genial earth,
Memories of bridal, or of birth,
And unto myriads more, of death.

O, wheresoever those may be,
Betwixt the slumber of the poles,
To-day they count as kindred souls;
They know me not, but mourn with me.

Everyone who has experienced the anniversary of the death of a
loved one will know already what Tennyson is going through,
but it is instructive and, I hope, helpful to see how he approaches
it. The first thing to notice is that the whole poem is addressed
to the anniversary day itself, as though that day were a person:
someone to be met with, blamed, praised, pleaded with and
learned from. Just look at the verbs used about the day itself,
at all the things the day itself is doing: it rises, it trembles, it
murmurs a song, and finally it wakens memories. The day has
become almost human, and in one sense it stands in the poem
as a proxy for the poet himself, and for us, his readers; we in
our different griefs must also rise, tremble, murmur our songs of
loving lament and waken our memories, however bitter-sweet.
But in another sense the day is an antagonist, an intruder whose
murmured music is, at least to the poet, a 'song that slights' his
'coming care'.

In the first verse Tennyson seems to be rebuking the day for
having the temerity to rise at all: 'Risest thou thus, dim dawn,
again'? Or perhaps it is that the dawn rises indifferent to its riot of
beauty, with its loud dawn chorus, its lowing herds and flowing
brooks, and the great trees touched with the fire of autumn. But
surely even as he rebukes the day he gives voice to its beauty and

sees that the fiery autumn woods he walks through on this day are not slighting his care, but are 'woodlands holy to the dead'. And it is with that insight – that all the beauty we see, even in our grief, can be consecrated as a tribute to our belovèd – that the tone and meaning of the poem, and so of the day, begin to change. For what the day does next is waken the memory with its 'balmy breath', and it is not just Tennyson's private memory that has been awakened. Suddenly the day itself lifts him out of the isolation of his grief and the poem opens out to include others for whom this day is the anniversary of loss:

> Who wakenest with thy balmy breath
> To myriads on the genial earth,
> Memories of bridal, or of birth,
> And unto myriads more, of death.

Tennyson sees at last, and allows us to see, all the 'myriads' going through this day with us. It is not that his grief is lessened, but it is companioned: he is lifted out of himself to wish a blessing and feel a kinship with others:

> O, wheresoever those may be,
> Betwixt the slumber of the poles,
> To-day they count as kindred souls;
> They know me not, but mourn with me.

Now we know why we have been invited to read the poem and share Tennyson's grief. For we are kindred souls with him; we mourn with him, and in turn his poetic gift enriches our mourning.

As as we read the poems in this part, and indeed in this whole anthology, I hope we will discover that in sharing the grief of others our own grief finds expression and we are able to bear it better.

20

Flower Rota

David Scott

This is my week for flowers.
It half says so on the damp notice in the porch.
(I had to borrow the pen from the Visitors' Book
and the ink ran out before my name.)
A few, who have let fall into their hearts
similar tragedies to mine, know why I chose this week
When flowers are hard to come by.
Each year I tell the season by a bowl of flowers,
whether things are late or soon, and predict
with those who visit here while I arrange,
the future course of summer.
They don't know for whom I struggle
to get this stalk through the chicken wire,
and it doesn't matter. When they are gone,
names half written in the Visitors' Book,
I'll have a moment when it's just
The flowers, the memory, and the sweet time it took.

There is so much to praise in this delicately wrought vignette.
We can see all the quiet, understated details; the damp notices
in the porch, the pen that doesn't quite work, the half-written
names in the flower rota. It draws our attention to a part of
a church's community life that is often taken for granted: the
flower arrangers whose work is so easy to overlook. We so often

assume that the church only comes alive when it is full on a Sunday, when the official service is happening, but this poem looks at the quiet ministry of those who slip in at odd times, keeping things tidy and making the place loved and lovely. And it observes too the way the place itself ministers to them. We feel that we are drawn close to the narrator as she speaks to us openly, intimately; we have become one of the 'few' who know why she arranges the flowers in this bleak season. She addresses us as those who like her have let tragedy 'fall into their hearts'. The word 'let' is important, implying openness, acceptance, a kind of chosen vulnerability. Gradually we realise that it is not just for the church as a community but for someone in particular whose memory, whose 'year's mind' she is keeping, that she struggles to arrange her few flowers just so. And the small outward 'struggle' with the chicken wire and the flower stems is a deft outward sign of that inward struggle with the remembrance of things past and the persistence of grief. And yet there is something fitting and right about it; the time it takes to struggle with the flowers is a 'sweet time', and taking the time is a sign of the love that makes it sweet.

And then, though we have been admitted to this intimacy, we see the gentle conventions of deflection; when others visit the church, those who 'don't know', she chats with them about the weather, about how the summer will be when it comes. Then the poem closes with that understated moment of stillness in the deserted church

when it's just
The flowers, the memory, and the sweet time it took.

David Scott, who included this poem in his beautiful collection *Playing for England*, is a poet-priest in the Church of England, a faithful pastor and a writer of great distinction, and one senses the years of priestly quiet, compassion and observation that lie behind this little piece. This poem became an inspiration for my own sonnet 'A Last Beatitude', but my debt of gratitude to the poet goes deeper, for when I was in my late teens and had just adopted a stance of defiant atheism David Scott arrived as chaplain at my school. He made time and space for me, took an interest in my reading, never judged me, was always gently suggesting and opening possibilities through which the divine might glimmer. He modelled for me what it might be like to be a 'grown-up poet', and when later I too became a priest, his example shone even more strongly. I am glad to share his work with his permission and to pay tribute to him here.

21

A Sudden Goldfinch

Holly Ordway

The branch is bare and black against the fog;
Cold droplets bead along the twigs, and fall.
The hours are passing, ready to be gone,
And now they're past, dissolved, beyond recall,
Beyond my reach. A sudden goldfinch clings
And bends the twig so slightly with its weight
It seems as if it's painted on: its wings
In motion are a glimpse of summer, bright,
Quick, and now already gone. This moment,
So brief but still so clear against the blur
Of unattended time, in memory
Connects the things that are, the things that were.
Fleeting as it is, almost a ghost,
It may be time is never truly lost.

Holly Ordway's sonnet is, like David Scott's poem, a delicately
wrought vignette, a particular moment of time that might have
flickered and gone, captured for ever in the amber of poetry.
Though it is not strictly about bereavement, it is a meditation on
time and memory that may well be helpful in this collection of
poems on the remembrance of things past. We start with the dark
and wintery image, the cold droplets beading and falling from a
bare branch in the fog, as though they embody the inevitably
passing hours, each hour gathering like a drop, and then gone,
falling way to nothing

ready to be gone,
And now they're past, dissolved, beyond recall,
Beyond my reach.

And then comes the 'sudden goldfinch'! It's beautiful the way it alights suddenly, halfway through the line, as though the line itself were the branch on which it perches, and it seems to bring with it another time, one with another quality altogether, with its sudden flash of colour and movement after the dull, clocklike falling of the cold drops:

its wings
In motion are a glimpse of summer, bright,
Quick, and now already gone.

Those words, 'bright, quick and now already gone', seem to me to recall two other moments in poetry when the sudden stirring of a bird does something strange to time. Ordway may be recalling Eliot's lines in the *Four Quartets* when the sound of a bird and of children laughing amid the leaves of a tree suddenly quickens him to a moment when time touches eternity and he cries, 'Quick, now, here, now, always'. But she may also be thinking of C. S. Lewis' lovely poem 'What the Bird Said Early in the Year', when on hearing a bird sing in Addison's Walk Lewis feels for a moment that eternity is beckoning:

This year, this year, as all these flowers foretell,
We shall escape the circle and undo the spell.
Often deceived, yet open once again your heart,
Quick, quick, quick, quick! – the gates are drawn apart.

Certainly the promise hidden in these two earlier poems quickens Ordway's own perception of the sudden moment when a bird brought its glimpse of summer. And so she attends to the moment in her poem, and allows us to do so too. She does not let it fall away to the long blur of 'unattended time' but sees instead how memory, as it makes and repairs our lost connections, can in some way redeem time for us, or point to the hope that time can be redeemed, that it will not finally pass 'beyond recall, beyond my reach':

> memory
> Connects the things that are, the things that were.
> Fleeting as it is, almost a ghost,
> It may be time is never truly lost.

What does this mean for us on the journey through grief? It means that the act of remembering is not in vain, that some moments may be so timeless that they become gates or windows beyond time. Somewhere, as our mortal love does its remembering, Love himself, Immortal Love, opens a window in our memory through which a light from beyond time streams in. God's grace may alight at any moment on the bare branches of our grief, as sudden as a goldfinch.

22

Parlour

Pádraig Ó Tuama

A year ago today Fr Gerry died.

The first day I met you, you asked questions
in the parlour for an hour –
our history started then, and the rest is story.
And it's the evening now, you're gone,
and I am full of mourning.
You held onto everybody's hand with your big hands –
soft skin, warm and some kind of kindlight in your eyes,
some small poem always hovering on the lips,
always anxious that righteousness and peace could kiss,
always moved to the truest truth that love can be woven
into all of this, all of this.
And even though it's still the evening
and I'll be grieving for a while, the morning light you lit
is burning like a fire, all around, all around.

In this lyrical and moving sonnet the contemporary Irish poet
Pádraig Ó Tuama commemorates, as in the extract from *In
Memoriam* in the Introduction, a first anniversary of loss. Like
Tennyson, he does so by directly addressing the person who has
died, and that itself, for all the grief one may feel, is an act of
hope, a trust that the separation of death is not final. As an anni-
versary piece the poem is full of the signs and markers of our life

in time: 'The first day ... for an hour ... it's the evening now ...
for a while ... morning light'. And time itself – the time shared,
parted and departed from – is one of its themes, and so the key
words, folded into one another, are 'history' and 'story': 'our
history started then, and the rest is story'.

But balanced against the divisions of time and time passing is
a counter-movement, a kind of gathering inclusiveness signalled
in the words 'always' and 'all', so that memory of someone who
'always moved to the truest truth' becomes woven with another
and deeper Love who sustains and blesses 'all of this, all of this'.

Amid these deeper themes the poem also gives us a particular
and vivid picture of a warm-hearted and generous person with
his big hands, the 'kindlight' in his eyes and a 'poem always
hovering on the lips', a man it seems with a particular ministry of
bridge-building and reconciliation. The poet remembers Father
Gerry speaking the words of Psalm 85.10–11:

> Steadfast love and faithfulness will meet:
> righteousness and peace will kiss each other.
> Faithfulness will spring up from the ground,
> and righteousness will look down from the sky.

One has the impression of a person always kindling lights and
warmth for others, preparing them for a greater light to dawn,
and so the poem moves, not as might be expected, from morning
to evening but, as in the creation story in Genesis, from evening
to morning. That movement is anticipated by a gentle word play
on mourning/morning:

> And it's the evening now, you're gone,
> and I am full of mourning.

Towards the end of the poem 'mourning' is itself redeemed by
the promise of morning:

> even though it's still the evening
> and I'll be grieving for a while, the morning light you lit
> is burning

And we finish with a sense, perhaps of the communion of the saints, of being surrounded by a great cloud of witnesses, lights in their several generations:

> the morning light you lit
> is burning like a fire, all around, all around.

23

Surprised by Joy

William Wordsworth

Surprised by joy – impatient as the Wind
I turned to share the transport – Oh! with whom
But Thee, long buried in the silent Tomb,
That spot which no vicissitude can find?
Love, faithful love, recalled thee to my mind –
But how could I forget thee? – Through what power,
Even for the least division of an hour,
Have I been so beguiled as to be blind
To my most grievous loss! – That thought's return
Was the worst pang that sorrow ever bore,
Save one, one only, when I stood forlorn,
Knowing my heart's best treasure was no more;
That neither present time, nor years unborn
Could to my sight that heavenly face restore.

We may be surprised to find a poem with 'Joy' in the title, here in the midst of an anthology intended to express and accompany grief. But of course it's the moments of joy, moments that we long naturally to share with the belovèd but cannot, that can so suddenly and piercingly remind us of our loss, and that is precisely the subject of this famous poem. Wordsworth perfectly expresses that strange experience in bereavement where despite knowing that someone has died, and that we have said good-bye, they are so deeply interwoven with our lives, the person to whom we would naturally turn to share our appreciation of all that is around us, that we find ourselves momentarily forgetting that we can no longer do so. For months, even years after we've lost them, we may turn to speak to them, wanting to share some thought or insight, only to find with a sudden bitter pang that they are not there – and we wonder, how could I have forgotten, even for a moment, that I have lost you?

So Wordsworth opens his sonnet:

> Surprised by joy – impatient as the Wind
> I turned to share the transport – Oh! with whom
> But Thee, long buried in the silent Tomb,

The phrase 'share the transport' may puzzle some modern readers. We still occasionally speak of being 'transported' with joy, and the Latin roots of the word make its inner meaning clear; 'trans' means 'through' and 'port' is rooted in the Latin word meaning to 'carry', so in this early sense to be 'transported' means to be carried through or beyond something. We can see how it soon applied its mundane sense to the transport of our bustling traffic, but Wordsworth is using the word far more deeply. At the very core of Wordsworth's poetic vision is the insight that moments of sudden joy have the power to lift us and move us through the veil of ordinary experience; they bring us to the brink of an experience that transcends the ordinary world we usually inhabit. He famously described this effect of joy in his poem written above Tintern Abbey:

> that blessed mood,
> In which the burthen of the mystery,
> In which the heavy and the weary weight
> Of all this unintelligible world,
> Is lightened: – that serene and blessed mood,
> In which the affections gently lead us on, –
> Until, the breath of this corporeal frame
> And even the motion of our human blood
> Almost suspended, we are laid asleep

In body, and become a living soul:
While with an eye made quiet by the power
Of harmony, and the deep power of joy,
We see into the life of things.

And this seeing deeply 'into the life of things' is also perceiving
through and beyond them to something transcendent, yet still
'deeply interfused' with all we see:

And I have felt
A presence that disturbs me with the joy
Of elevated thoughts; a sense sublime
Of something far more deeply interfused,
Whose dwelling is the light of setting suns,
And the round ocean and the living air,
And the blue sky, and in the mind of man:
A motion and a spirit, that impels
All thinking things, all objects of all thought,
And rolls through all things.

Wordsworth's masterpiece *The Prelude* is about how these
visitations, these moments when joy suddenly surprises us, are
connected together like a golden thread drawing us sweetly and
strongly towards the divine mystery out of which all things arise
It is for this reason that C. S. Lewis, who enjoyed many of these
Wordsworthian 'transports' of joy, chose to call his spiritual
autobiography *Surprised by Joy*.

It was also characteristic of Wordsworth that he wanted to
'share the transport'. That is what makes him a poet: his desire
and his power to share these experiences, to help us have them
too. As lovers of his work will know, he does that brilliantly in
his poetry. We have only to walk with his poetry in our hands,
or better still in our hearts, to find that we too are sharing his
transports, and with the deep power of joy, seeing into the life
of things.

But Wordsworth asks 'with whom' is he to share this particu-
lar moment of surprising joy, and the answer to that question

deepens his poem further for us. This sonnet was written some time after Wordsworth's belovèd daughter Catherine died, and it is almost certainly to her that he had found himself turning, with her he had hoped to 'share the transport'. Catherine Wordsworth died just before her fourth birthday, in 1812. The whole Wordsworth household adored her; she had brought a sense of fun and joy to them all. Indeed Wordsworth had earlier written a beautiful poem about her called 'Characteristics of a Child Three Years Old':

> Loving she is, and tractable, though wild;
> And Innocence hath privilege in her
> To dignify arch looks and laughing eyes; ...
> who fills the air
> With gladness and involuntary songs.
> Light are her sallies as the tripping fawn's
> Forth-startled from the fern where she lay couched;
> Unthought-of, unexpected, as the stir
> Of the soft breeze ruffling the meadow-flowers

So we get a sense that Catherine herself was often 'surprised by joy', as well as surprising her father with the joy she gave him. But there is another special thing about her that has been uncovered by the research of the scholar-poet Grevel Lindop. Lindop believes that Catherine had Down's syndrome:

> How do we know that Catherine had Down's Syndrome? It's not certain but it is extremely likely. I noticed the evidence when I was researching the life of the essayist Thomas De Quincey, and a couple of years ago pointed it out to Muriel Strachan, who is writing a book on the Wordsworth children, and suggested she examine the evidence systematically. She did so and the case seems very clear.
>
> Catherine was born when the poet and his wife were both 38. A loveable and delightful child, she was said by Dorothy Wordsworth to have 'not ... the least atom of beauty', but a wonderful sense of humour and 'something irresistibly comic

in her face and movements'. Wordsworth used to call her 'my little Chinese maiden' – probably relating to the epicanthic fold of skin which gives some Down's children an unusual shape to the eye. She seems to have had heart problems and suffered from convulsions and some problem with swallowing. All these symptoms point very strongly to Down's Syndrome.*

Anyone who has had the pleasure of getting to know a Down's syndrome person, and particularly a child, will recognise the tremendous gift they have for communicating joy and a sheer sense of fun, the irresistably comic, the light 'sallies', the unexpected bursts of merriment.

And so Wordsworth, in a sudden and unexpected moment of joy, naturally turns to share it with little Catherine who was so much part of his life, only to find that she is gone. He is taken suddenly from that joy to a deep realisation of his 'most grievous loss' and to another memory, the moment at her graveside:

when I stood forlorn,
Knowing my heart's best treasure was no more;
That neither present time, nor years unborn
Could to my sight that heavenly face restore.

Though Wordsworth grieves that nothing will restore to him the sight of her face, yet the very act of remembering, and the making of the poem itself, a beautifully crafted Petrarchan sonnet, becomes a kind of restoration. There is a sense in which this little girl has helped Wordsworth recover the childlike transports of joy he so much valued, keeping alive the child within the man. Perhaps it is no accident that the poem, for all its sadness and lament, begins with joy and ends with the word 'restore'.

---

* Grevel Lindop, 'Catherine Wordsworth: A Romantic Poet's Downs Baby', https://grevel.co.uk/andanotherthing/catherine-wordsworth-a-romantic-poets-downs-baby/

24

Remembrance Sunday Afternoon

Malcolm Guite

November sunlight shimmers on the Wear,
Wide waters slip unhurried by each bank
And soothe Remembrance Sunday afternoon.
After the service, after the parades,
After the poppies, after the last post,
I sit and drink in quietness and peace,
The peace those Durham infantry forsook
To keep it sacred for the likes of me.
Some of them surely fished this very spot
Where Durham fishermen are sitting still
On folded campstools. May those fallen men
Whom we remembered in the high cathedral
Drink deep now from the river of true life
Where all their wounds are healed, where living light
Flows from the source of every time and tide
And may they know that we remember them.

Although this poem is not about a moment of either surprise or
forgetfulness it does in some ways continue the theme of how
to hold our present experiences of calm or peace or beauty in
tension or in harmony with our memories of those who cannot
share that peace with us now.

I wrote this poem on Remembrance Sunday in Durham in 2014
when I was staying there as a visiting fellow at St John's College.

Perhaps it was because I experienced the familiar Remembrance service in an unfamiliar place, and because it was the Remembrance Sunday that fell exactly 100 years after the beginning of the war that changed so much for so many and whose impact we still feel, that Remembrance that year seemed especially poignant. I had been to the service in the cathedral which had been a great and solemn occasion, with civic and church dignitaries in full regalia and, more movingly, many serving members of the armed forces in their uniforms, remembering not just the fallen of the two world wars, which were once the only focus of this day, but also those of more recent conflicts. Afterwards, again because of the centenary, there was a large parade down the winding way from the high cathedral into the town, of young men, just the age of the Durham infantrymen who went off to the war 100 years before, marching past us wearing the uniforms and carrying the arms of the period. It was like being transported for a moment back in time, and we who stood at the side of the road cheering them on became one for a while with the families who had waved goodbye to their loved ones in 1914 to a war from which so few returned.

Later I sat by the River Wear on that bright November afternoon to gather my thoughts. It was, as I suggest in the poem, a deeply peaceful and tranquil scene and I noticed that among the young men fishing quietly on the banks were some I had seen wearing the uniforms earlier, and it was from that that the poem emerged. I had a strong sense of the peace, the simple and quiet things of life that soldiers leave behind when they are sent to war. I knew that the peace of these quiet places is all the more precious because it has been preserved by the sacrifice of those who did not return.

But there was more than that. I longed that those who had forsaken this peace should have it restored to them, and so I found myself in prayer, and in that prayer being 'transported', drawn in and through the light on the river before me to that other river of light we glimpse in Revelation 22.1–2:

Then the angel showed me the river of the water of life, bright as crystal, flowing from the throne of God and of the Lamb through the middle of the street of the city. On either side of the river is the tree of life with its twelve kinds of fruit, producing its fruit each month; and the leaves of the tree are for the healing of the nations.

I had the sense that everything flows from that true and healing source. I imagined the men who had left the banks of the river here 100 years ago, away upstream now, on the banks of that heavenly river, in the place where their wounds are healed.

The last line of the poem, 'And may they know that we remember them', touches, I think, on a deep need, a deep hope that we have as bereaved people that in some way our own remembrance, our continued love for those who have died, may be a blessing on them. That is why, like so many others, I often pray the prayer:

Rest eternal grant unto them, O Lord,
and let light perpetual shine upon them.

PART 5

Letting Go

With the tolling of a bell we enter the strong, slow rhythm of letting go

Introduction

We move now from the bitter-sweet remembrance of things past and come gradually, perhaps tentatively, to the place where we can begin to do some letting go. For, as we said in the Introduction to this anthology, it is when the remembrance of things past, which is a kind of holding on, has begun its healing work, then there can also be, paradoxically, a letting go. Not that we ever let go of love or memory or even grief, but gradually we are able to let the one we love go back into the heart of God from whence they came. It is never an easy or a simple process nor is there a single moment when we can say that we have done it, although the funeral service tries, in vain, to provide us with one. It is much more like a series of moments, a cycle or circle of releases, like the tolling of a bell or the repetitive pattern of an oft-recited childhood prayer. Once again, Tennyson's *In Memoriam* may help us to see something of the meaning and character both of this staging post on our journey and of the landscape beyond it. We will take up the thread of his grief journal in Section LVII, which is a real turning point of the whole piece. From Sections L to LVI Tennyson gives vent to his anger and fear about the apparent pointlessness of life and the cruelty and violence of nature. In Section L he speaks of being

> rack'd with pangs that conquer trust;
> And Time, a maniac scattering dust,
> And Life, a Fury slinging flame.

And Section LVI, which includes the famous phrase 'red in tooth and claw', finishes with a plea that he should move past that impasse and hear another voice. Its final stanza reads:

> O life as futile, then, as frail!
> O for thy voice to soothe and bless!
> What hope of answer, or redress?
> Behind the veil, behind the veil.

Then comes a complete change of tone and voice. The lovely Section LVII seems to come as an answer, from 'behind the veil', to the desperate pleas the previous section closed with.

> Peace; come away: the song of woe
> Is after all an earthly song:
> Peace; come away: we do him wrong
> To sing so wildly: let us go.
>
> Come; let us go: your cheeks are pale;
> But half my life I leave behind:
> Methinks my friend is richly shrined;
> But I shall pass; my work will fail.
>
> Yet in these ears, till hearing dies,
> One set slow bell will seem to toll
> The passing of the sweetest soul
> That ever look'd with human eyes.
>
> I hear it now, and o'er and o'er,
> Eternal greetings to the dead;
> And 'Ave, Ave, Ave,' said,
> 'Adieu, adieu,' for evermore.

Perhaps it is because he has dared to voice his turmoil and confusion so boldly in the preceding sections that Tennyson's muse is able to speak a real and deep peace into his soul: not a quick fix or cheap grace but a peace that somehow includes and also transforms or transposes the sorrow it follows. You have sung your song of woe, the first two verses seem to be saying; now come away, leave the graveside awhile. The repeated phrase 'let us go' sounding out in the first two verses seems to carry an implicit message: let Arthur go too.

But even as the muse draws him away and speaks peace, we hear Tennyson saying, as anyone would in his place, 'But half my life I leave behind'. Letting our belovèd go into God is hard, partly because it is letting part of ourselves go too. Even as he leaves the graveside, Tennyson reflects on his own mortality, and even the mortality of these verses with which he hoped to enshrine his friend.

> Methinks my friend is richly shrined;
> But I shall pass; my work will fail.

Had this section ended here it might have led Tennyson back to the place from which he was trying to escape, struggling with a sense of futility. But the music of the poem surges forward and becomes the rich, rhythmic chiming of a bell sounding in honour of the dead and making new music for the living. It is the solemn chiming of this 'One set slow bell' that prepares Tennyson for the celebrated passage of true release that comes later in the poem: 'Ring out, wild bells, to the wild sky' (Section CVI). For now the music of the poem tolls simply and beautifully, the single syllables of that line, 'One set slow bell will seem to toll', sounding singly and sonorously. Then we have the repeated bell-like music in the final verse of 'o'er and o'er', 'Ave, Ave, Ave', 'Adieu, adieu', and the last chiming of the long rhyme on 'evermore'. That lovely final verse also contains a delicate and telling echo of a much earlier poet, the music of whose Latin verse is summoned to sing and ring through Tennyson's English. Tennyson is here recalling some famous lines of Catullus, from his wonderful elegy *'Frater ave atque vale'*. The lines are given below in Latin so that you can hear the sound of them, followed by a translation.

Accipe fraterno multum manantia fletu,
Atque in perpetuum, frater, ave atque vale.
Take them, wet with many tears of a brother,
and for ever, O my brother, hail and farewell!

Tennyson wrote of these lines, 'Nor can any modern elegy, so long as men retain the least hope in the after-life of those whom they loved, equal in pathos the desolation of that everlasting farewell.'

So we hear Catullus in Tennyson's repeated 'Ave, Ave', but then he makes a subtle change, which discreetly whispers the Christian hope Catullus never had. For the last word here is not '*vale*' (farewell) but 'Adieu, adieu' (to God, to God). So it can be for us: 'Adieu, adieu for evermore' seems so final and hard to say, but hidden in the words is the name of God to whom we commend those we let go. Now we let them go to the God who, in the end, is there for us too.

25

Prayer

Carol Ann Duffy

Some days, although we cannot pray, a prayer
utters itself. So, a woman will lift
her head from the sieve of her hands and stare
at the minims sung by a tree, a sudden gift.

Some nights, although we are faithless, the truth
enters our hearts, that small familiar pain;
then a man will stand stock-still, hearing his youth
in the distant Latin chanting of a train.

Pray for us now. Grade 1 piano scales
console the lodger looking out across
a Midlands town. Then dusk, and someone calls
a child's name as though they named their loss.

Darkness outside. Inside, the radio's prayer –
Rockall. Malin. Dogger. Finisterre.

T. S. Eliot said that Tennyson had the best ear for music of any
English poet, but this poignant sonnet seems to me to catch, keep
and sound again some of the best music in English poetry. It
reads so naturally, yet keeps the full pattern and rhyming sound
of the Shakespearean form with its three quatrains and couplet.
This itself is apposite and telling, since the poem is about the

healing effect of remembered patterns of sounds and repetitions. The poem comes to us like a gift, and it is itself about the gift in those moments when 'although we cannot pray, a prayer utters itself'. It is in these moments that, little by little, almost unaware, we can let go of our grief.

Duffy gives us a series of glimpses, vignettes of the gift being received, the prayer uttering itself through us just as the repetitive bell sounded through Tennyson's verse. As each moment comes and a new truth enters us, there is a little lift. So in the first quatrain the woman lifts her head from her hands at the song in the tree; in the second, the man stands stock-still hearing 'the distant Latin chanting of the train. Pray for us now.' This phrase tells us exactly which Latin prayer from his youth he hears in the sound of the train. 'Pray for us now' comes from the prayers of the rosary, itself a soothing, almost mechanically repeated pattern of prayer: '*Ora pro nobis nunc et hora mortis nostrae*' (Pray for us now and at the hour of our death). Like Tennyson, Duffy summons the Latin without needing to say it. But it is still there as a hidden music under the English words, like the railway track under the train carriage. The poem has taken us back to the pattern of childhood now, and so the lodger, hearing a child playing scales somewhere in the house, is consoled and connected again with his own childhood. The poem touches again on our grief as dusk comes, and so much is intimated in the deft lines, 'someone calls a child's name as though they named their loss'.

As we come to the final couplet we realise that the poet has been taking us quietly through the course of a day, and now we come beyond dusk to 'midnight and close down', the late-night shipping forecast: the litany of repeated names becomes the radio's prayer. In the last rhyme sounds of 'prayer' and 'Finisterre' we return, as though circling through rosary beads, to the sound with which the poem opened.

This is not specifically a poem about grief or 'letting go'; rather it is about unconscious prayer, prayer as a gift from an unknown giver. Yet it seems that just such moments as this poem describes are when our 'letting go' and healing release actually happens.

26

Threnody

Scott Cairns

The dream is recurrent, and yes
the dream can leave me weeping,
waking with a start, confused,
and pressing my wet face hard
into the pillow. That is to say
the dream is very bitter.

The scenes are various, the gist
unchanging: my father returns,
and we all are at once elated
that his death was apparently
an error, that he had simply
been away, a visit to the shore.

Then, increasingly, I grow
uneasy about how deeply
he has changed. He is both frail
and distracted (or it could be
that he withholds some matter
focusing his mind), and none of us

dares speak, neither of his death nor
of his sudden, startling return.
We share other confusions as well:
He has arrived in the camper truck
he drove when I was a boy, but my wife
and children are also here to greet him,

even my son, whom he has never met.
Often, in the dream, I am the one
who first suspects he cannot stay.
I am the one who sees but cannot say
his visit will be brief. And just
as I suspected, as I feared, I wake.

Tennyson and Carol Ann Duffy in their different ways may
have lulled us into thinking that this business of letting go can
be gentle, steady, gradual, and it will happen without too much
trauma in those unattended moments when the bell tolls and the
prayer prays itself: alas, it is not so. There are jolts and shudders
and turning back, and the bitter realisation that we haven't
let go yet. There are moments like the one we saw in Part 4
when Wordsworth turns to share his joy with Catherine, only
to remember with a shock that he has let her go into the grave
and has more letting go to do. So too with this tender but sear-
ingly honest confession of a difficult recurring dream from Scott
Cairns. In Part 1 we were with Cairns as he said goodbye to his
father on the very threshold of his dying; now, sometime later,
we see how much work there is for the living to do.

A threnody is a song of lamentation; the word is taken from
the Greek *threnodia* (from *threnos*, dirge or lament, and *oide*,
ode). And so this poem begins not simply with the dream but also
with weeping, with 'pressing my wet face hard into the pillow'.
The dream, like many of our stages of grief, is recurrent: we keep
having to go back and repeat what we thought we had accom-
plished. The pain, the bitterness of which the poet speaks, comes
from the sheer alternation of hope and grief. Many bereaved
people will have had the experience not only of dreaming of
the person but apparently seeing them; they may glimpse them
in peripheral vision, or in a stranger's face. This experience is
described in both of the Thomas Hardy poems we have looked
at. These recurring dreams carry with them the uncanny sense
that we have been through all this before, and we despair at the

idea of having to go through it again. But a dream is also a gift. We know that something is being worked out through it. One of the most moving things in Cairns' account of his dream is the way his living family, particularly the son his father never met, are in the dream with him. It is as though all that the poet has now become, even since his father's death, must be brought to bear on the real work of letting his father go. It is interesting, too, that in the dream it is the poet himself who takes responsibility for this bitter and difficult task of letting go:

> Often, in the dream, I am the one
> who first suspects he cannot stay.
> I am the one who sees but cannot say
> his visit will be brief.

Perhaps each time the dream recurs a little more of the letting go is done. Perhaps this too is the work of the threnody itself as a poetic form. Its Ancient Greek root *threnos* shares older origins with Proto-Indo-European languages, in words that have come down to us through Old English. One of those, *dran*, gives us our word drone, the word that describes that continuous repetitive sound we hear in some early forms of music, especially the Gaelic lament. The drone of the bagpipe grounds the higher, skirling, wailing notes of the tune; the drone string on a stringed instrument gives rhythm and harmonic grounding to other elements in the music. Perhaps there is also something of the rhythmic, repetitive work of the worker drone going on in the darker cycles of pain that still accompany our recovery, and in the new music we need to make with the rest of our lives.

There is something richly ambivalent in the final words of the poem :

> ... And just
> as I suspected, as I feared, I wake.

At one level this is bleak and cheerless; the poet doesn't want to wake. He is afraid of losing his father again. But still the last

word of the poem is 'wake', and that word carries with it for
every Christian something of the dawn, a promise, the resur-
rection. It carries echoes of the great proclamation in Ephesians
5.14:

Sleeper, awake!
Rise from the dead,
and Christ will shine on you.

27

Holding and Letting Go

Malcolm Guite

We have a call to live, and oh
A common call to die.
I watched you and my father go
To bid a friend goodbye.
I watched you hold my father's hand,
How could it not be so?
The gentleness of holding on
Helps in the letting go.

For when we feel our frailty
How can we not respond?
And reach to hold another's hand
And feel the common bond?
For then we touch the heights above
And every depth below,
We touch the very quick of love;
Holding and letting go.

This little poem had a particular beginning and a strange after-life. When my father was in his late seventies, and not very well, it happened that a lifelong friend of his who was just the same age died suddenly. I knew him too and it was a shock to all of us, and I very much wanted to be with my father when he went to his friend's funeral. I think for both of us this death was an intimation of my father's mortality. Time spent with my father was very precious then, but on the day itself a pastoral crisis arose in the college where I am chaplain and I had to be there in the midst of the emergency and I missed the funeral. But before the funeral I was able to have lunch with my father and we were joined by a very good friend of mine who also knew my father well, and she went to the funeral with him; she was going on my behalf. They walked away together towards the church, and as I was getting on my bike to go up to the college I glanced at them. Just as they turned a corner to go out of view I saw my friend reach out and hold my father's hand. She had done just the right thing, what I would have liked to do – but actually wouldn't have done had I been there. Afterwards, when I had dealt with the situation in college, I sat down in a café to write my friend a thank you card, and also wrote this little poem for her.

It was so particular and so much of the moment that I didn't think it was a 'keeper', or that it would necessarily say much beyond the intimate moment that gave it birth. But I showed it to my wife, who sent it to a friend, who shared it with someone who worked in a hospice, and she in turn read it to a group of her fellow hospice workers at their morning prayer meeting. A week later I received a letter saying that my poem had expressed for them the heart of their philosophy and approach as a hospice. They felt that approach was summed up in the lines:

> The gentleness of holding on
> Helps in the letting go.

This came as a surprise, but when I read the poem again with their eyes I saw entirely what they meant. So I included the poem in my collection *The Singing Bowl*, and later got occasional letters from people who had found it helpful, had used it at funerals or sent it to the recently bereaved.

I learnt from this that the poet is not necessarily the best judge of what is happening in a poem or what it is ultimately about. Or rather, that poems are like children; you nurture and form them up to a certain point, and of course you have your own ideas about what they mean and who they are. But they are living independent beings; like children growing up and leaving home, published poems go out and make their own way in the world, they make new friends and have conversations their parents could never have imagined and perhaps shouldn't overhear. But sometimes they come home with their new friends and you have the pleasure of knowing that someone has seen something in your child, in your poem, that you hadn't seen yourself, but you are very glad it's there.

So now I send this poem out again, and giving it a place in this anthology in the hope that it might teach and share more than I know myself about the gentleness of holding on, and the art of letting go.

28

Rest Lake

Michael Ward

The jetty stretching out into the lake
Is straight and hard beneath the wind and sleet;
On left and right the winter shorelines arc
To lock a rattling shackle where they meet.
The jetty's a stamen in a beeless bowl,
A barbed arrow, lodged hard in a heart,
A bridegroom rigid in a sad girl's soul:
I reach its end and squat and look about.
Around me, trees stir; above me, clouds tower;
Below me, clouds and trees wave in the lake.
I sigh and sit, reflecting hour by hour,
And seek the very centre of my ache.
I sit and wait. I wait and sit until
The skies and lakes are clear, the trees are still.

There is a stillness and clarity about this sonnet, which is itself about stillness and clarity. Michael Ward is best known as an expert on C. S. Lewis and the author of *Planet Narnia*, a book that demonstrates in how many subtle ways Lewis' knowledge of medieval astrology informed and deepened the imagery of his Narnia series. But here Ward turns to verse and in a sonnet whose metre and rhyme follow the Shakespearian form of three quatrains and a couplet he gives us a concentrated meditative sequence of attention, tension and release. The poem describes a visit to a lake in Finland near the village of Lepojarvi, whose name translates as 'rest lake'.

As the poet approaches the lake, with its lone jetty stretching out towards its centre, we have a sense of something harsh and austere, almost forbidding. The jetty is 'straight and hard beneath the wind and sleet'. The 'winter shorelines arc' round in front of and behind the poet as he begins to walk along the jetty as though a 'rattling shackle' were closing to lock around him. And this rattling shackle is the first in a series of gradually changing images of the lake and its jetty each reflecting and in some way moving the inner state of the narrator.

One intuits, even at this point, that the poet has come to the lake because he is in some way stuck; something is locked in him and needs release, needs letting go. As he approaches the end of the jetty in the lake this outward and visible place is becoming a series of inward and spiritual emblems. In the next image, 'The jetty's a stamen in a beeless bowl', we have the sense of disconnection and absence, of frustrated potential. The stamen is the pollen-producing part of the plant but it requires the bee to pollinate. Something is wrong, something is missing. The next image takes us further: 'A barbed arrow, lodged hard in a heart'. Now the lake, which was a shackle, and the bowl of a flower, has become a heart, but one pierced with a barbed arrow. We are dealing not just with absence but with a piercing pain, a hurt with barbs that make it difficult to dislodge. But more subtly, as the jetty becomes the arrow that pierces the lake-heart, we have a sense that as the poet walks out towards the centre of the lake he is walking in towards the centre of his own heart.

Then comes the last in this sequence of four images, each taking us a little deeper into the pain that has drawn the poet to rest lake: 'A bridegroom rigid in a sad girl's soul'. This is a powerful and I think deliberately ambiguous image. In one way we could read it as being about human relationships and heartache in the conventional sense, the 'bridegroom rigid in a sad girl's soul' suggesting a kind of paralysis or even death. The one she would have welcomed in her soul has somehow become only a frozen image. The poem might be read in that way, but then we know that it is a man and not a woman who is offering us this image, or feeling it as he contemplates the jetty in the lake.

And that opens up another and perhaps richer possibility. Following a tradition deeply rooted in scripture, the mainstream of Christian spiritual writing has often represented Christ as he comes to rescue us with his love as the Bridegroom, and the Church, and the individual Christian soul too, as correspondingly the Bride. St Bernard of Clairvaux in his commentary on the Song of Songs, for example, represents his own soul as the Bride and Christ as the Bridegroom who seeks her, and whom she seeks in her turn. We are to welcome Christ into our souls as the bride welcomes the bridegroom into the garden in the Song of Songs. C. S. Lewis continued that tradition in his own poetry and spoke of his soul as feminine, asking in one poem, 'Oh who will reconcile in me both maid and mother?' Ward would certainly be deeply aware of this tradition.

On this reading we might see these successive images – the shackle, the unpollinated stamen, the wounded heart, the girl's sad soul – as cries of the spirit, expressions of being spiritually stuck, bound or unfruitful. The fourth image of the bridegroom rigid in the soul may suggest that the poet has at some point accepted Christ into his soul but somewhere, on the journey he has allowed that inner Christ to become 'rigid', fixed and frozen: an image of past devotion, not the presently living, breathing, risen Christ. It may be that grief or depression has seemed for a while to freeze even the deepest religious impulses and experiences. If this is the case then here is a poem that is longing for release and resurrection. One might say that spiritually it is located on Holy Saturday: the agony of some personal Good Friday has happened and now in the strange, seemingly locked and frozen quietness of the following day the numbed soul feels the wound of absence and the Bridegroom himself seems dead to her. We are in that strange, quiet, empty place between the pain of Good Friday and the joy of Easter Sunday.

We are now at the end of line 7, the midpoint of the sonnet, and the poet brings us back from the inner to the outer. We see him outwardly reach the end of the jetty, and inwardly seek the centre of his still unnamed ache:

> I reach its end and squat and look about.
> Around me, trees stir; above me, clouds tower;
> Below me, clouds and trees wave in the lake.
> I sigh and sit, reflecting hour by hour,
> And seek the very centre of my ache.

We become aware of the reflective power of the lake itself, of the way the things out there and above, the clouds and trees, are reflected in the depths below, and then that word 'reflect' is taken up perfectly to describe what the poet is doing and what has already been going on in the poem. Just as the clouds are reflected in the lake's depth, so all these outer images, of the cupped bowl of the lake and the straight jetty, the journey along it to a centre, have reflected the inner spiritual opening that is taking place here in the rest lake.

We began with movement and disturbance, with wind and sleet, the poet moving along the jetty, the trees stirring in a wind that must surely have disturbed the lake's surface. Now we come to a centre where we can indeed rest and wait for stillness and clarity:

> I sit and wait. I wait and sit until
> The skies and lakes are clear, the trees are still.

That penultimate line is itself a kind of mirroring and reflection, in the chiasmus of ' I sit and wait. I wait and sit'. And then at last we come to the still centre: 'The skies and lakes are clear, the trees are still.' The last word is 'still', and it summons up the line from scripture, 'Be still, and know that I am God'. This may be the stillness, perhaps, of Holy Saturday, but it is an expectant stillness. One feels a promise that in that still reflection, hour by hour, something is going to be resolved, released, and the bridegroom, no longer rigid, will arise in the soul.

29

Scattering the Ashes

Grevel Lindop

At last the rain cleared and we found a barley-field
where the crop was knee-high, and in our town shoes
paced the lumpy furrows along the edge
until our trousers were soaked. My brother held it out,
open, and I pushed my hand in. It was like
dark corn, or oatmeal, or both, the fine dust
surprisingly heavy as it sighed through the green
blades and hit the earth. And like the sower
in that nursery picture ('To bed with the lamb
and up with the laverock') we strode on, flinging it
broadcast, left and right, out over the field.
And there was no doubt that things were all in their places,
the tumbled clouds moving back, light in the wheel-ruts
and puddles of the lane as we walked to the car;
and yes, there were larks scribbling their songs on the sky
as the air warmed up. We noticed small steps
by a pool in the stream where a boy might have played
and people fetched water once, and wild watercress
that streamed like green hair inside the ribbed gloss of the
     current.
And then I was swinging the wheel as we found our way
round the lane corners in a maze of tall hedges
patched with wild roses, under steep slopes of larch
and sycamore, glimpsing the red sandstone of castles
hidden high in the woods. And the grit under our nails

was the midpoint of a spectrum that ran from the pattern in
    our cells
to the memories of two children, and it was all right.

It seems good to conclude this part on 'Letting Go' with a poem
about the literal letting go involved in scattering ashes. In this
vivid, vigorous account of scattering his father's ashes, Grevel
Lindop offers us something more than a particular personal
story, for even as he gives us so much earthy and individual
detail he seems to body forth for us more universal feelings, and
intimations about completion, rightness and renewal, about the
new beginnings enfolded in our ending.

We start the poem with the words 'At last', which seems
appropriate, for the scattering of ashes is something that usually
happens well after the funeral, the committal at the crematorium;
there has been a chance to gather the particular family members
who need to be there and to find the place that seems in every way
right for the scattering, perhaps even one chosen by the deceased.
So the poet and his brother are together for this last goodbye and
letting go; the field has been found, the rain has cleared and we
are ready. We get the sense of the journey they have made in the
little comment about their 'town shoes' pacing the 'lumpy fur-
rows along the edge' of a country field, the barley field full of all
that is green and growing – the grain that in its turn will make the
bread, the staff and sustenance of life. At first, almost as though
the poet is reluctant, the flask or scattering urn in which the ashes
are contained is not named. We are simply told

My brother held it out,
open, and I pushed my hand in.

But once the scattering begins there is a detailed vivid account,
appealing to all our senses: to touch and sight and hearing, so
clearly that it is almost as though we were there, feeling it all
with the poet:

It was like
dark corn, or oatmeal, or both, the fine dust
surprisingly heavy as it sighed through the green
blades and hit the earth.

And here it is the analogy itself, not simply the description that
carries us into the deeper meaning of the poem. We stand in the
field of young and growing barley and now the ashes themselves
are 'like dark corn, or oatmeal', and it is through the 'green
blades' that they hit the earth. There may be an echo here of the
Easter hymn:

Now the green blade riseth from the buried grain,
Wheat that in the dark earth many years hath lain;
Love lives again, that with the dead hath been:
Love is come again, like wheat that springeth green.

Certainly, the poem goes on to draw on the biblically resonant
image of the sower:

And like the sower
in that nursery picture ('To bed with the lamb
and up with the laverock') we strode on, flinging it
broadcast, left and right, out over the field.

Lindop summons a nursery picture of the sower out early, which
must have been captioned with the Scots saying, 'Gae tae bed wi'
the lamb and rise wi' the laverock' (laverock is a Scottish dialect
word for a lark which was also widely used in English until the
nineteenth century) – one of many variants about retiring and
rising early. It's a particular memory, no doubt, but in this new
context of scattering ashes it gently hints, as some of our other
poems have done, at death as a kind of sleep and resurrection as
a waking to new life.

Lindop, like a number of other poets in this collection, is not
a Christian and he does not directly cite here the parable of the
sower, nor the other words of Jesus: 'Very truly, I tell you, unless

a grain of wheat falls into the earth and dies, it remains just a single grain; but if it dies, it bears much fruit' (John 12.24). Nevertheless, his poetry is richly open and available to the Christian reader, in whose mind these biblical associations will be naturally implicit, though they are not forced on us in any way. But the poet is certainly wanting us to share the feeling he and his brother have that this scattering of their father's ashes is indeed a kind of sowing, a letting go that will in the long run be fruitful. He continues:

> And there was no doubt that things were all in their places,
> the tumbled clouds moving back, light in the wheel-ruts
> and puddles of the lane as we walked to the car;
> and yes, there were larks scribbling their songs on the sky
> as the air warmed up.

It is not just the fittingness of these beautiful natural details and how his memory of the laverock is answered and fulfilled by the larks in the sky; his father's return to the earth is itself right and fitting, that the ashes of his body should be let go back to the earth from which they came, to become part once more of the growing processes out of which our bodily lives are formed and nurtured.

And so the poem turns naturally to see with new clarity all the signs of life, to help us receive their beauty and promise and be blessed by them. The 'small steps by a pool', left by a playing child, seem fitting after letting go of someone at the other end of life. The lovely image of the watercress streaming under the ribbed gloss of the current, the glimpses of wild roses, of larch and sycamore, all these both speak of a return to the green goodness of the earth and suggest the gracious cycles of new life and growth. And this rich sense of rightness, of depth and connection with the world in which we live and the long continuation of growth and renewal that are patterned in the rings of a tree and in plant cells as much as they are in the generations of a family, is all brought together in the beautiful lines that conclude the poem. We realise that even though the ashes have been scattered

and let go, their little trace in 'the grit under our nails' is a sign
that at a deeper level, in memory, in the way the two brothers
live and renew their lives, they will also keep and continue all
their father has given them:

> And the grit under our nails
> was the midpoint of a spectrum that ran from the pattern in
>   our cells
> to the memories of two children, and it was all right.

PART 6

Receiving

*The veil lifts, we glimpse the goodness
of things deepened and sharpened
by sorrow*

Introduction

In the last poem of Part 5 we saw how the gradual letting go, literally and emotionally expressed in the scattering of ashes, richly opened the poet to receive the sights and sounds offered in the field where the ashes were scattered. This section of the book is about that stage in our journey when we are opened and able to receive again, when the icy marble statue we glimpsed in Elizabeth Barrett Browning's poem 'Grief' has wept its tears at last and is free to move. It is not that we cease to sorrow, but that sorrow itself opens us with a new and poignant sensitivity to all that life still has to offer rather than closing and blinding us. Our memories, which may be as vivid as ever, have become companions on our forward journey rather than shades pulling us back.

As in each of these introductions we can find some helpful words and images in Tennyson's *In Memoriam*. So let us hear from late in the sequence, from Section CXV, the way another spring, this time the third since his loss, comes to the poet.

> Now fades the last long streak of snow,
> Now burgeons every maze of quick
> About the flowering squares, and thick
> By ashen roots the violets blow.
>
> Now rings the woodland loud and long,
> The distance takes a lovelier hue,
> And drown'd in yonder living blue
> The lark becomes a sightless song.

Now dance the lights on lawn and lea,
The flocks are whiter down the vale,
And milkier every milky sail
On winding stream or distant sea;

Where now the seamew pipes, or dives
In yonder greening gleam, and fly
The happy birds, that change their sky
To build and brood; that live their lives

From land to land; and in my breast
Spring wakens too; and my regret
Becomes an April violet,
And buds and blossoms like the rest.

We come to this most musical and beautiful evocation of spring, a recognition of a spring within us as well as without, and we can trust the gift and grace it offers. By this time readers of *In Memoriam* are deep into a sequence of poems that has dared to give honest voice to the dark, ghastly and broken side of grieving, and because we have gone through so much with Tennyson, we are able to understand and receive what this section has to offer. Taken out of context, these verses might seem, like the oft-quoted extract from Henry Scott Holland, to be no more than sentiment and wishful thinking. But in their true context we can trust the hope they bring.

The first thing to note is that Tennyson himself and his grief for Arthur Hallam, which have been so obsessively the subject of the work so far, don't actually come into this section until the final verse. That itself is part of the healing. Tennyson, in letting Arthur go, is also able to loosen the icy grip on his own pain. It fades like 'the last long streak of snow' of the opening line, and makes way for the blessing of spring. Grief may still be there, like the 'ashen roots', but beside it spring the violets, to which we will return in the final verse. The opening verse also sets the tone of vivid presence, beginning as it does with 'Now', as does each of the first three verses. The verbs too tell their own story.

'Now burgeons every maze of quick': burgeons is set there as the perfect regenerative opposite of 'fades' in the first line. The 'maze of quick' uses 'quick' as a country shortening of quick-set thorn, but it carries its earlier Prayer Book sense of the living as in the contrast of 'the quick and the dead'.

Then after 'burgeons' as the key verb in the first verse, we get 'rings' in the second, with its evocation not only of the loud music of the wood but also of the more exquisite and distant 'sightless song' of the lark. Tennyson, and also Lindop in the last poem, would have been aware as they brought skylarks into their poems of Shelley's vision of the lark as a liberated spirit:

Hail to thee, blithe Spirit!
Bird thou never wert,
That from Heaven, or near it,
Pourest thy full heart
In profuse strains of unpremeditated art.

Once we have read Shelley's 'Ode to a Skylark' the flight and song of the bird must always speak of a blithe spirit ascending to sing at heaven's gate.

Then in Tennyson's third verse the 'now' verb becomes 'dance', and we get the sense of the lights glancing off the land, the flocks on the hill and the sails on the sea, all in their different ways lightening and dancing for the poet and inviting him to be lit within and also lightened of his load. In the fourth verse these leading verbs suddenly themselves burgeon into a whole flock of verbs: 'pipes ... dives ... gleams ... fly ... change ... build ... brood ... live': a cluster of eight quickening verbs all rushing along in four short lines. That verse ends with a phrase that must surely reflect life back to the poet, for what the spring calls the birds to do is 'live their lives' and so Tennyson must begin again to live his. The poem turns to its liberating conclusion in the final lines:

and in my breast
Spring wakens too; and my regret
Becomes an April violet,
And buds and blossoms like the rest.

It is not that regret has disappeared, but it has taken a new and helpful form: not the grasping and shadowing 'churchyard yew', but an 'April violet' that can bud and blossom. The poems in this part of our anthology are chosen to reflect and enable that transformation to new and more helpful modes of loving lament. Indeed two of them are by poets we saw earlier in this collection, returning to the theme of their grief but in a new way.

30

The Double Crown

Adrian Rice

Sometimes I feel like I let you down in
The end, old friend, spending time out running
Around with other best friends. I guess I
Never learned from the late neglect of my
Lonely grandmother. Funny, last word I
Shared with her over the phone was Jesus.
Just in case I'm right – if I let us
Down in life – I hope you'll accept poetry
In the hereafter as poor recompense
From the man you mentored who's seen some sense.
So take this double crown (wreathed at each end)
And you wear yours, and I'll wear mine
And let's break bread together across space and time;
Me, in the here-now; you, in the there-then.

This is the final poem, the epilogue, in Adrian Rice's sonnet
sequence 'The Moongate Sonnets', written in memory of his
neighbour Billy Montgomery. We looked at the second sonnet
in this sequence, 'The Grieving Ground', in Part 3 in which Rice
sees his friend trying to shoo away a blackbird whose noisy pro-
test turns out to be a lamentation for its mate. But the bird can
no more shoo that grief away than Billy can let go of his grief for
his wife, and neither can Rice lose his own grief for Billy. The
various sonnets in the sequence visit other moments of memory

from the course of their friendship. The tenth sonnet, 'The Last Look', remembers Billy's last glimpse of a place he loved, the following two record the funeral and then a dream after Billy's death in which at last these two reticent and understated men say something of what they feel. The title of the epilogue, 'The Double Crown', is an allusion to 'La Corona' (The Crown), a famous sequence of seven sonnets by John Donne; as this is Rice's final sonnet in the sequence, it completes two 'coronas' and is therefore a 'double crown'. Over the course of the poem, the double crown itself becomes a symbol of something much more, of a friendship that reaches 'across space and time' and beyond death.

Rice starts the poem with a confession that will be familiar to anyone who has been bereaved: the sense of regret, the persistent but no doubt irrational feeling that one should or could have done or said more, spent more time with the person one has lost. That regret calls up and summons other regrets, other losses:

> Sometimes I feel like I let you down in
> The end, old friend, spending time out running
> Around with other best friends. I guess I
> Never learned from the late neglect of my
> Lonely grandmother.

The tone here is as of simple direct conversation with the friend he has lost. Then almost casually, offhand it would seem – in the oblique manner of Ulster – he drops in the most important word of all, the name that will make sense both of the dying and of the chance of a continued communion beyond it: Jesus. It was his last word to his grandmother and now it becomes the first word in a covenant with his old friend, for that is what the second half of the poem is: a renewed friendship with the memorial poetry, itself, as a pledge.

> I hope you'll accept poetry
> In the hereafter as poor recompense
> From the man you mentored who's seen some sense.

This part of the anthology is about the bereaved and grieving at last being able to receive, but we begin, paradoxically, with a grieving man offering something that might be received by the dead, however poor a recompense it might be. The whole sonnet sequence is offered to Billy as a 'double crown (wreathed at each end)', 'wreathed' picks up the sense of a funeral wreath, but 'at each end' is important too, for one 'end' is in the mind of the living poet and the other is a gift to the soul of the departed. So this turns out not to be a funeral wreath, but a living thread of connection. Both men are crowned, one with honour and the other with memory and, almost as though it were a childhood game, Rice tells his friend 'you wear yours, and I'll wear mine'. Then comes the real covenant and communion between the friends, which Jesus himself makes possible for he is equally present on either side of Charles Wesley's 'narrow stream of death'. Rice concludes his double corona with the lovely lines:

And let's break bread together across space and time;
Me, in the here-now; you, in the there-then.

All this is said in the most simple and lucid language. There is no religious jargon, no talk of mortality or immortality, or things temporal and things eternal, not even the churchy words I have used in my account of the poem, words like covenant and communion: just clear, uncomplicated phrases like 'break bread together'. Earth and heaven are simply the 'here-now' and 'there-then'. We know, as we read this, that the grieving man who is offering these poems to his departed friend is also receiving something far greater in return.

31

Friends Departed

Henry Vaughan

They are all gone into the world of light!
And I alone sit ling'ring here;
Their very memory is fair and bright,
And my sad thoughts doth clear.

It glows and glitters in my cloudy breast,
Like stars upon some gloomy grove,
Or those faint beams in which this hill is drest,
After the sun's remove.

I see them walking in an air of glory,
Whose light doth trample on my days:
My days, which are at best but dull and hoary,
Mere glimmering and decays.

O holy Hope! and high Humility,
High as the heavens above!
These are your walks, and you have show'd them me
To kindle my cold love.

Dear, beauteous Death! the jewel of the just,
Shining nowhere, but in the dark;
What mysteries do lie beyond thy dust
Could man outlook that mark!

He that hath found some fledg'd bird's nest, may know
At first sight, if the bird be flown;
But what fair well or grove he sings in now,
That is to him unknown.

And yet as angels in some brighter dreams
Call to the soul, when man doth sleep:
So some strange thoughts transcend our wonted themes
And into glory peep.

If a star were confin'd into a tomb,
Her captive flames must needs burn there;
But when the hand that lock'd her up, gives room,
She'll shine through all the sphere.

O Father of eternal life, and all
Created glories under thee!
Resume thy spirit from this world of thrall
Into true liberty.

Either disperse these mists, which blot and fill
My perspective still as they pass,
Or else remove me hence unto that hill,
Where I shall need no glass.

The seventeenth-century poet Henry Vaughan had a conversion experience and renewal of faith as a direct result of reading George Herbert's poetry; he wrote that he owed to Herbert his 'spiritual quickening and gift of gracious feeling'. Like Herbert and the other 'metaphysical' poets Vaughan delights in paradox, and in the sudden discovery of meaning or insight in unlikely places. But he was also a visionary, capable of a rapturous apprehension of heaven (he wrote a poem that opens 'I saw Eternity the other night') and, as we see in this poem, of discerning the way the light of heaven glimmers and beckons even through the things of this world, and especially through the people we love here.

The poem starts with the assurance that his departed friends are in the light of heaven, and one might think that this would lead to a simple, almost dualistic contrast between light there and darkness here; the second line, 'I alone sit ling'ring here', might seem to suggest that, but it is not so. Vaughan's memory of his friends is a light in this world, an inner light that is not just in heaven above but also 'glows and glitters in my cloudy breast'. It shines like the tiny points and beams of starlight above a darkened hill:

> Their very memory is fair and bright,
> And my sad thoughts doth clear.
>
> It glows and glitters in my cloudy breast,
> Like stars upon some gloomy grove,
> Or those faint beams in which this hill is drest,
> After the sun's remove.

But this is only their memory. The friends whose departure he mourns have their true being in the light of heaven, and the contrast seems only to emphasise the shadowed and trampled world in which Vaughan still finds himself.

> I see them walking in an air of glory,
> Whose light doth trample on my days:
> My days, which are at best but dull and hoary,
> Mere glimmering and decays.

The poem is oscillating between moments of vision and lapses back into a sense of darkness and melancholy, yet Vaughan knows these glimmerings and intimations have been shown to him in order to 'kindle' his 'cold love'. And then in the fifth stanza comes the beginning of a genuinely transfigured vision. He sees Death in a new light, as a dust-covered jewel which, like some magical gem in a romance, opens a door to mysteries beyond itself:

Dear, beauteous Death! the jewel of the just,
Shining nowhere, but in the dark;
What mysteries do lie beyond thy dust
Could man outlook that mark!

'Could man outlook that mark!' This compressed and beauti-
ful line requires a little opening out. 'Outlook' here means
'look again' or 'look beyond'. And 'mark' carries the sense of
an archer's mark, the target at which he takes aim. The whole
effort of Vaughan's poetry is to offer us a new way of looking,
and also 'outlooking'. The first part of the poem has looked at
the mark of death, not just in the metaphor of the archer taking
aim, but in the deeper sense of the 'mark' of death; the way we
are all marked by grief for friends departed and fear of our own
death. But now Vaughan's art summons us to 'outlook', to look
through and beyond, the mark of death. For Death is a mark
in another sense; it is a sign. The marks in ink on the paper
that make up the poem are themselves signs for words, and the
words the signs of the vision; we 'outlook' the mark to find the
word, 'outlook' the words to read the poem, and then 'outlook'
the poem to see the vision to which it points. And so Vaughan
is inviting us to read death not as a full stop but as a word in
God's poem, something through or beyond which we look at the
mysteries which 'do lie beyond' that dust.

He begins to give us this double vision, this sense of the pos-
sibility of a presence even in the midst of an observed absence,
with the image of an empty nest:

He that hath found some fledg'd bird's nest, may know
At first sight, if the bird be flown;
But what fair well or grove he sings in now,
That is to him unknown.

The key phrase in this stanza is 'At first sight'. By reminding us
of what is knowable from a first glance he is preparing us, by
implication, for that second sight, the outlooking, that is at the
heart of this poem. He gives us the imagined possibility of the

unknown but actual 'well or grove' in which the fledgling sings. As bereaved people all we see at first are a series of 'empty nests', vacancies and blank spaces where our belovèd used to be; but this poem asks us to go beyond 'first sight', to outlook that mark, and at least to imagine the 'fair well or grove' where the flown bird still sings.

And now Vaughan moves from the analogy of the fledged bird's nest to a direct address to the soul, an appeal beyond a rational knowledge of the outer to an intuitive knowledge of the inner, suggesting that the inner yearnings are not echoes in the cave of our lostness, but rather callings from heaven itself.

> And yet as angels in some brighter dreams
> Call to the soul, when man doth sleep:
> So some strange thoughts transcend our wonted themes
> And into glory peep.

Then, after all these hints and foreshadowing, comes the key image, which has been hinted at in the idea of something fair and bright glittering 'in my cloudy breast', and again in the idea of the jewel 'Shining nowhere, but in the dark': that of the buried star:

> If a star were confin'd into a tomb,
> Her captive flames must needs burn there;
> But when the hand that lock'd her up, gives room,
> She'll shine through all the sphere.

Vaughan has come a long way from the simple and desolate contrast between light above and darkness below with which the poem opened. In the very act of grieving he has discovered afresh the captive flames of his own immortal soul. And now death, which at the beginning of the poem had robbed him of his friends, has become instead the hand that will give him liberty. After loving lamentation he is at last ready to receive, ready to speak directly to his Father, able to rejoice in eternal life without despising the glories of time. True, he prays for liberation from this world, but it is a prayer that acknowledges that God's light can shine through the creation as well as beyond it, and that sometimes that light will disperse the mists that blot and fill the glass through which we darkly see the world. The final line of the poem, 'Where I shall need no glass', is a reference to the recently invented 'perspective glass', as the telescope was then called: the instrument that enhances vision and allows us to 'out-look' our usual mark. Indeed, Vaughan's poetry has exactly that effect on our 'perspective', in both its old and modern senses. Vaughan closes his poem with a prayer to the 'Father of eternal life', asking that if he cannot now find himself in heaven, he may have the mists dispersed so that he may 'peep' into glory. In some ways the answer to that prayer is the poem itself; the power of the poetic imagination to clear away the mist and allow us at least a glimpse of glory:

O Father of eternal life, and all
Created glories under thee!
Resume thy spirit from this world of thrall
Into true liberty.

Either disperse these mists, which blot and fill
My perspective still as they pass,
Or else remove me hence unto that hill,
Where I shall need no glass.

32

Lucencies (2)

Michel Faber

You worked covertly,
nurturing by stealth.
You lifted people up,
nudged them to transcend
their limitations,
in sickness and in health.
Those you assisted looked around
to thank you, but you'd hide.
When your influence began to spread
too far, you died. I still hear
your whisper in my ear:
'Let's be going.'

If I could scan this planet
with X-rays that detect the presence
of your timely interventions,
I'm sure I'd find them
In places you would not expect.
You're dead. I know. And it is not for me
To show you death is not the end.
But you left lucencies of grace
secreted in the world,
still glowing.

We return now to the work of Michel Faber; we read the first of
his two 'Lucencies' in Part 1 of this anthology. That first poem
explored the incongruity between words, beautiful and mel-
lifluous themselves, that are used in the medical realm of cancer
and cancer treatment, and the painful or deadly things to which
they actually refer. So the word 'lucencies', which he called 'the
most beautiful' of all those technical words, describes 'those pale
glows revealed by radiography'. But what the lucencies revealed
were 'ghostly holes': the work of the cancer. At the very end
of his book *Undying: A Love Story* (for this is its final poem)
recording the long journey from shock through loving lament
and the bitter-sweet remembrance of things past, Faber returns
to the word 'lucency' and is able to receive something new and
redemptive from it. Indeed, there is a redemption of language
going on throughout this poem. It is addressed directly to Eva
herself:

> You worked covertly,
> nurturing by stealth.

These opening lines themselves are a redemption, a reversal of
what the cancer had been doing to her. That too worked 'covertly'
and 'by stealth', not to nurture but to destroy, not to lift up but
to break down. This first stanza describes an experience, a series
of discoveries, that will be familiar to many bereaved people and
often a great and perhaps surprising comfort to them: the gradual
revelation of all the previously unknown good that their belovèd
has done. Stories of quiet virtues, hidden good deeds, little
gifts and graces, sometimes start to appear in the conversation
directly after a funeral and may continue in the letters of comfort
that we receive. When my father died, my mother and I began to
discover through comments and letters from far and wide how
many people he had helped, the good he had done, how students,
fellow church members, even comparative strangers had been
touched in ways we had never known. So it is for Faber in this
poem, and he addresses his deceased wife in telling these happy
discoveries:

> You lifted people up,
> nudged them to transcend
> their limitations,
> in sickness and in health.

The poignant echo of the marriage vows in that last phrase acknowledges both the unspoken good she has done him and also how that good was spread more widely. The tribute to Eva's modesty, in doing so much anonymously, slipping away before she could be thanked, continues to reverse and redeem the image of the covert cancer:

> you'd hide.
> When your influence began to spread
> too far, you died.

Here her death itself, caused by the spreading influence of the malign and hidden cancer, is reread as a humble withdrawal, leaving a benign and spreading influence for light and life.

The second half of the poem returns to the image of the X-ray scan that came at the end of the first 'Lucencies' poem. But this time it is not an image of the body of a woman where, in ironic lucencies, the presence of cancer is detected; this time it is a spiritual X-ray of the world revealing in real and beautiful lucencies that woman's 'timely interventions' for good in other people's lives. They show up unexpectedly as little points of light in our darkened world, as ' lucencies of grace'. This discovery of the light of someone's life not transcendently above in a heaven of light but 'secreted' in the world is very like the insight we had from Henry Vaughan in the previous poem; the memory of his friends who have 'gone into the world of light' is still, paradoxically, generating a light for Vaughan in this world: 'it glows and glitters in my cloudy breast, like stars'. Vaughan was a mystic and a man of strong Christian faith; Michel Faber, as we read earlier, does not have that comfort. He is clear and lucid about that absence of faith throughout his book, and yet just as he ended the first 'Lucencies' poem with the word 'shine', so now he holds together the sheer brutal fact of his loss and the continuing light of Eva's life, letting each of these truths speak to the other in whatever way they can through the mind of his reader.

> You're dead. I know. And it is not for me
> To show you death is not the end.
> But you left lucencies of grace
> secreted in the world,
> still glowing.

There is a wonderful, self-deprecating agnosticism in the lines paradoxically addressed to the dead, 'And it is not for me to show you death is not the end.' But somehow the statement 'death is not the end' shines strongly through, itself a lucency at the end of a poem whose last word is 'glowing'.

33

A sequence from *Adonais*

Percy Bysshe Shelley

XXXIX

Peace, peace! he is not dead, he doth not sleep,
He hath awaken'd from the dream of life;
'Tis we, who lost in stormy visions, keep
With phantoms an unprofitable strife,
And in mad trance, strike with our spirit's knife
Invulnerable nothings. We decay
Like corpses in a charnel; fear and grief
Convulse us and consume us day by day,
And cold hopes swarm like worms within our living clay.

XL

He has outsoar'd the shadow of our night;
Envy and calumny and hate and pain,
And that unrest which men miscall delight,
Can touch him not and torture not again;
From the contagion of the world's slow stain
He is secure, and now can never mourn
A heart grown cold, a head grown gray in vain;
Nor, when the spirit's self has ceas'd to burn,
With sparkless ashes load an unlamented urn.

XLI

He lives, he wakes – 'tis Death is dead, not he;
Mourn not for Adonais. Thou young Dawn,

Turn all thy dew to splendour, for from thee
The spirit thou lamentest is not gone;
Ye caverns and ye forests, cease to moan!
Cease, ye faint flowers and fountains, and thou Air,
Which like a mourning veil thy scarf hadst thrown
O'er the abandon'd Earth, now leave it bare
Even to the joyous stars which smile on its despair!

XLII
He is made one with Nature: there is heard
His voice in all her music, from the moan
Of thunder, to the song of night's sweet bird;
He is a presence to be felt and known
In darkness and in light, from herb and stone,
Spreading itself where'er that Power may move
Which has withdrawn his being to its own;
Which wields the world with never-wearied love,
Sustains it from beneath, and kindles it above.

XLIII
He is a portion of the loveliness
Which once he made more lovely: he doth bear
His part, while the one Spirit's plastic stress
Sweeps through the dull dense world, compelling there
All new successions to the forms they wear;
Torturing th' unwilling dross that checks its flight
To its own likeness, as each mass may bear;
And bursting in its beauty and its might
From trees and beasts and men into the Heaven's light.

XLIV
The splendours of the firmament of time
May be eclips'd, but are extinguish'd not;
Like stars to their appointed height they climb,
And death is a low mist which cannot blot
The brightness it may veil. When lofty thought
Lifts a young heart above its mortal lair,

And love and life contend in it for what
Shall be its earthly doom, the dead live there
And move like winds of light on dark and stormy air.
...

LII
The One remains, the many change and pass;
Heaven's light forever shines, Earth's shadows fly;
Life, like a dome of many-colour'd glass,
Stains the white radiance of Eternity,
Until Death tramples it to fragments.

The first extract from *Adonais*, which we read in Part 3 of this
anthology, ended with Shelley expressing the almost unbearable
contrast between the joyful renewals of spring and his experience
of irrecoverable loss. How can it be, Shelley asked, that when the
beauties of the earth renew themselves each year, the one beauty
that is able to know and praise the other beauties should be lost
for ever? We left him 'feeling the contradictions, pressing the
questions, restlessly questing for answers'. In this extract, taken
from towards the end of the work, we find him able to receive
some answers. The strong tensions of the earlier passage are
transmuted here into a powerful and generative paradox. We,
the living, think of ourselves as fully alive and of the dead as lost
and diminished, but perhaps it is the other way around! Perhaps
those who have died have stepped into a glory of which we have
seen only glimmerings, have awakened to a life of which we have
only dreamt. In the first extract Shelley wept to think of Keats
as the 'leprous corpse', but now he sees it another way; it is we
who decay like corpses and Adonais/Keats who has by contrast
'out-soar'd the shadow of our night'. In stanza XLI, this al-
legedly atheist poet presses on to an insight that is familiar from
scripture and in the work of Christian poets like John Donne,
that death itself shall die: 'He lives, he wakes – 'tis Death is dead,
not he'. And now Shelley calls on Nature herself, so celebrated in

both his own verse and that of Keats to express the transcendent life of her young poet:

> Thou young Dawn,
> Turn all thy dew to splendour, for from thee
> The spirit thou lamentest is not gone;

Shelley, while he was scarcely the atheist he claimed to be, was emphatically not a Christian and does not acknowledge, in this poem, how it is and by whose power and grace death has been overcome; yet he recognises that in and through nature there is a loving power at work, which had a care for Keats. Some people have read the famous lines at the beginning stanza XLII as entirely pantheistic:

> He is made one with Nature: there is heard
> His voice in all her music, from the moan
> Of thunder, to the song of night's sweet bird;

That is to say, asserting that nature is God, God is nature, and there is nothing more beyond that; in dying we return to the cycles of nature's growth and are therefore still there in some form, but there is no 'beyond', no Mind or Love transcending nature. This is not what Shelley is saying in *Adonais*, as the final lines of this very stanza make clear. For Shelley there is a Power beyond nature 'Which has withdrawn his being to its own'. This Power is not nature herself, but rather is one

> Which wields the world with never-wearied love,
> Sustains it from beneath, and kindles it above.

These are two of the most beautiful lines in the whole poem. Whatever Shelley's views, the Christian reader could scarcely find a better expression of the God Christ reveals to us, the Father whose 'never-wearied love' still 'wields the world', 'sustains ... and kindles it'; even more, who sustains, kindles and calls to his eternity those he has made in his own image.

Shelley was in fact not a pantheist but a Platonist. He believed in a transcendent realm of pure and eternal form that is, in some sense, veiled by the world of nature. Indeed, there is sometimes a danger in Shelley's language of a dualism in which the world is less a veil than something 'dull' and 'dense', a 'dross' that checks the spirit's flight. A stronger doctrine of creation and of God's glorious incarnation into flesh would have helped him here, but in fact his own deeper poetic inspiration, given I believe by the Spirit, comes to his aid instead. So the very stanza in which he speaks of 'the dull dense world' and the 'unwilling dross' nevertheless ends with the image of the power and unwearied love of the divine

bursting in its beauty and its might
From trees and beasts and men into the Heaven's light.

The final lines from this extract, in stanza LII, both express and redeem this dualism with the beautiful image of life as being 'like a dome of many-colour'd glass' through which the radiance of eternity is shining:

Life, like a dome of many-colour'd glass,
Stains the white radiance of Eternity,
Until Death tramples it to fragments.

In almost any other context the word 'stains' would carry the sense of the world as sin or contagion, but the one context in which the word is redeemed is stained glass. And here Shelley the 'atheist', expressing his deepest hopes, draws on the art and imagery of the Church he has left, for surely some childhood memory of a stained-glass window is being transformed here. So Shelley receives and offers to us the hope that when the beautiful but brittle glass of our own lives is trampled by death and shattered, the lights, the lucencies, that we have glimpsed in one another will shine with a new radiance.

34

I Went to Sleep at Dawn in Tuscany

Hilaire Belloc

I went to sleep at Dawn in Tuscany
Beneath a Rock and dreamt a morning dream.
I thought I stood by that baptismal stream
Whereon the bounds of our redemption lie.
And there, beyond, a radiance rose to take
My soul at passing, in which light your eyes
So filled me I was drunk with Paradise.
Then the day broadened, but I did not wake.

Here's the last edge of my long parchment furled
And all was writ that you might read it so.
This sleep I swear shall last the length of day;
Not noise, not chance, shall drive this dream away:
Not time, not treachery, not good fortune – no,
Not all the weight of all the wears of the world.

Hilaire Belloc (1870–1953) is now remembered mainly for his delightful children's verse – the *Cautionary Tales*, and *The Bad Child's Book of Beasts* – but Belloc was a man of many parts and a serious as well as a comic poet. Behind the biting political satire associated with his public persona, there was a man of deep feeling whose predisposition to melancholy was at once heightened and relieved by his even deeper sensitivity to beauty.

Belloc was to the very depth of his being a romantic, not just in theory but in practice. As a young man, trying to make a name and a life in letters in London, he glimpsed across a crowded room a beautiful red-haired Irish-American girl called Elodie Hogan (1868–1914) and fell in love with her. It was a love that remained constant for the rest of his life. She returned his feelings, but just as they were beginning to come to an understanding about their intentions her family took her back to California, almost certainly to get her away from the young man without money or prospects. Belloc's response was to brave the transatlantic journey in steerage and then walk from New York right the way across America, sleeping rough and earning money by making and selling quick sketches. He found his belovèd Elodie and won her hand just before she was about to be sent to a convent. He brought her back to England to make their lives together there. When Elodie died in 1914, Belloc went into mourning and continued to wear black from that day until his death in 1953.

Both Belloc and Elodie were strongly believing Catholic Christians but there was always, in Belloc, a kind of fighting, grim determination in his faith. He believed Christianity to be true and intellectually coherent and he accepted it on the authority of the Church but for long periods he hardly felt its inward consolations in himself. Elodie, by contrast, lived and breathed her faith and in particular her sense of the communion of saints and the grace of Mary. She seemed to be able to hold that faith for Belloc and bless him with it so that he loved her both for herself and for the way her life and faith constantly reflected to him the beauty and grace of heaven. Belloc wrote poems for her while she was alive and continued to do so after her death; they were published in 1923, nine years after Elodie's death, alongside other poems in his book *Sonnets and Verse*. As one reads through the sequence of poems for Elodie it is sometimes hard to tell whether a poem was written before or after her death; those written while she was alive are full of a sense of heaven, and those from after her death describe her present life in Christ and continued love for all whom she loved on earth.

This poem was, I believe, written after her death and is about one of those dreams of the belovèd that sometimes come to comfort the bereaved. The language of this sonnet is simple and yet elevated, intensely personal and yet resonant with the great themes of Christian redemption. The opening line, which brings sleep and dawn together and introduces a morning dream brings out this paradox. For this dream is no compensatory night-time delusion, but a premonition of the true morning and awakening promised in the resurrection. The figure of the poet standing on one side of the stream and glimpsing his belovèd on the other is archetypal but may also carry an allusion to Dante's *Divine Comedy*, which Belloc knew and loved. Dante, just before he actually encounters his belovèd Beatrice, dreams of a woman on the other side of a stream, a great light in her eyes. This stream is the baptismal stream not because baptism looks back to birth but because it looks forward to death and to resurrection. All Christians are baptised into Christ's death and his resurrection. We emerge from the font into this world and back into the arms of our mothers but we also emerge as children of heaven, already ritually crossing the stream between us and paradise.

But for now, even in the dream, Belloc, together with all mourners, is still on this side of the stream. Nevertheless, the radiance he sees 'there, beyond' on the far side of the stream passes over to this side and

> rose to take
> My soul at passing, in which light your eyes
> So filled me I was drunk with Paradise.

This supreme moment in the dream and the word 'Paradise' leads to the end of the octet of the sonnet. The sestet returns us to Belloc in this world. But he has received something, something that cannot be taken away, and he realises that at least one aspect of the dream will never leave him. He will not have to wake from it until he awakens from the dream of life itself into paradise. For this is not like the dream that troubled Scott Cairns in the poem 'Threnody', from which he must wake to confront his loss again and complete his letting go, rather this is an oracular dream of comfort and assurance, a gift from heaven.

The wonderful, emphatic final lines of this sonnet seem consciously to echo Paul's great affirmation in Romans 8.38–39:

> Not noise, not chance, shall drive this dream away:
> Not time, not treachery, not good fortune – no,
> Not all the weight of all the wears of the world.

> For I am convinced, that neither death, nor life, nor angels, nor rulers nor things present, nor things to come, nor powers, nor height, nor depth, nor anything else in all creation, will be able to separate us from the love of God in Christ Jesus our Lord

In this biblical allusion, Belloc is not misappropriating the text, for his vision of Elodie and paradise is not separated from their shared baptismal faith but is rather a fulfilment of it. From Belloc's perspective the rock beneath which he dreams his dream is the Church whose one foundation is Christ.

Another sonnet to Elodie from earlier in the sequence, which I believe was written while she was still living, shows very beautifully how their shared faith meant that even as Belloc loved her intensely in this world that very love could itself recognise and rejoice in the fact that her true home, and his, was really heaven. Her love, beauty and faith was constantly mediating this heaven to Belloc, and it seems right to conclude this reflection with that earlier poem.

Mortality is but the Stuff you wear

> Mortality is but the Stuff you wear
> To show the better on the imperfect sight.
> Your home is surely with the changeless light
> Of which you are the daughter and the heir.
> For as you pass, the natural life of things
> Proclaims the Resurrection: as you pass
> Remembered summer shines across the grass
> And somewhat in me of the immortal sings.

You were not made for memory, you are not
Youth's accident I think but heavenly more;
Moulding to meaning slips my pen's poor blot
And opening wide that long forbidden door
Where stands the Mother of God, your exemplar.
How beautiful, how beautiful you are!

35

Paradigm Shift: Angelus

Holly Ordway

Within the deepest silence is a sound:
Ordered, graceful, the music of the spheres
Reverberates in every atom, bounds
From star to star: a song we cannot hear,
Except in hints and glimpses: in the hush
Of twilight, crickets with their tiny words;
A smile upon a sleeping face; a rush
Of love within the heart; high circling birds
Against the burning blue of heaven; sparrows
Darting quick into the hedge; the air before
The rain and after; mossy bridges, furrows
At harvest: woven, a vast cosmic score
In secret sung. And we beneath the moon
Can add our prayers: sunset, sunrise, noon.

In the poem that concluded the previous commentary, Hilaire Belloc witnesses to the experience of seeing a light and beauty in this world that seems to glimmer through from a world beyond. Such a vision summons in us a hidden and unexpected music, which we are called to sing. As Belloc put it:

> as you pass
> Remembered summer shines across the grass
> And somewhat in me of the immortal sings.

The poem by Holly Ordway also speaks of the way in which beauties in this world become 'hints and glimpses' of the eternal, snatches of 'a song we cannot hear'. She sets these intimations of immortality, these moments of the eternal sounding into time, within the context of the ancient Christian idea of the perpetual song of praise of the angels and the related idea of the music of the spheres. This is the belief that all the parts of the cosmos are in some sense always singing, but it is only fallen mortal human beings who cannot hear the song, except in rare moments of grace. The Christmas carol 'It came upon a midnight clear' celebrates a moment when this heavenly song was heard by the shepherds. The carol goes on to lament:

And man, at war with man, hears not
The love-song which they bring:
O hush the noise, ye men of strife,
And hear the angels sing.

Perhaps Holly Ordway was thinking of that 'hush' when she suggests that it is 'in the hush of twilight' that we can begin to hear the song again.

In medieval and renaissance times the cosmos was perceived as a series of nested, crystalline spheres, each turned by an angel and making music as they move, hence Milton's famous lines:

Ring out, ye crystal spheres,
Once bless our human ears
If ye have power to touch our senses so ...

We no longer believe in that crystalline spheres model of the cosmos so Ordway, rather than simply adopting an outmoded cosmology, sets the music of the spheres within a modern understanding of our still beautiful and mysterious cosmos.

the music of the spheres
Reverberates in every atom, bounds
From star to star:

In fact, this is not far removed from one modern cosmological theory. String theory suggests that the perceptible cosmos framed in space and time arises as the harmonics of inconceivably tiny strings vibrate or sound through 11 dimensions. Although Ordway acknowledges and delights in the reverberation of tiny atoms she is really calling our attention, opening our eyes and ears, to the experiences we can all have of perceiving through the things of this world hints and glimpses from beyond. The smile on a sleeping face, the high circling of birds, sparrows in the hedgerow and the furrows at harvest: all of these are just small parts of a 'vast cosmic score in secret sung'.

But there is more – a deeper dimension still, and to understand this we must look to the clue given in the title, 'Paradigm Shift: Angelus'. The poem certainly offers a paradigm shift: a complete shift in the way we see things, appealing against a reductive, analytic modern approach that only sees the broken and deadened parts of our world and does not hear the harmony of the whole. And what of 'Angelus'? This is a reference to the Angelus bell, rung to remind people in the middle of their busy lives to stop and pray with the angels at dawn, noon and sunset. The prayer is called the 'Angelus' because it begins with a reference to the annunciation, when Gabriel came to Mary: '*Angelus Domini nuntiavit Mariae, et concepit de Spiritu Sancto.*' (The angel of the Lord declared unto Mary, and she conceived of the Holy Spirit.)

In the tradition of the Angelus prayers we cease to be passive spectators of this incarnation, but actively join our voice with the angels, willing with them that the love of heaven should reach us here, that we might so hear their song on earth that the hope is kindled anew and that we shall also join their song in heaven. We remember Mary's gracious 'yes' to God, and as we pray the Angelus we make it our own. This is why the Angelus and this delightful modern poem that celebrates it have their place in an anthology for those who mourn. We tend to associate the tolling of a church bell with the passing of a soul and a funeral, but once the sounding of a bell three times across the fields in the middle of the working day reminded all of us, including those who mourn, of the angel's song and the promise at its core. Heaven has come to earth in Christ, that we might come to heaven in him.

At the funeral of the great Irish poet Seamus Heaney, his son Michael told a wonderful story about the poet's last words and how they brought comfort to his grieving family. They had visited him in hospital and as he had seemed stable they had left; and when the crisis of his passing came upon him he was alone. He had a phone with him and was able just to text two words to his wife: '*noli timere*' (do not be afraid) – the very words of the Christmas angels when the music of heaven was heard again on earth: 'But the angel said to them, "Do not be afraid; for see – I am bringing you good news of great joy for all the people"' (Luke 2.10).

PART 7

Hope

We awaken to the hope of resurrection

Introduction

In Part 6 we saw that even as we grieve, we can receive hints, glimmers, anticipatory echoes of heaven, or simply of sheer goodness, which had been for a while veiled to us in our grief. In this final part we shall try to bring these hints and glimpses into the clear, strong focus of our hope in Christ: the hope of resurrection. So the opening poem is about the awakening of all Christian hope when dawn rose on the Easter garden and Jesus called a grieving woman by her name. But before we turn to that dawn, we will spend one last time sharing Tennyson's long journey towards hope in *In Memoriam*.

Sometimes it is quite literally an outward, physical act of moving on in our day-to-day lives that helps us to move on spiritually and emotionally. Towards the end of Tennyson's grief journal come a series of lyrics occasioned by the fact that he and his widowed mother were to leave the Rectory at Somersby where he had grown up. Most importantly for him, it was where his friend Arthur had spent summers with him, had fallen in love with Tennyson's sister, and where the two (or three) of them had roamed the meadows and streams while the first buds of poetic gifts in both men had begun to blossom. The night before they left the old house for good, Tennyson was granted one of those strange dreams that come to the bereaved, that seem to be more of an assurance of the future than a remembrance of the past. Here is how he tells the story in the hauntingly beautiful Section CIII of *In Memoriam*.

CIII

On that last night before we went
From out the doors where I was bred,
I dream'd a vision of the dead,
Which left my after-morn content.

Methought I dwelt within a hall,
And maidens with me: distant hills
From hidden summits fed with rills
A river sliding by the wall.

The hall with harp and carol rang.
They sang of what is wise and good
And graceful. In the centre stood
A statue veil'd, to which they sang;

And which, tho' veil'd, was known to me,
The shape of him I loved, and love
For ever: then flew in a dove
And brought a summons from the sea:

And when they learnt that I must go
They wept and wail'd, but led the way
To where a little shallop lay
At anchor in the flood below;

And on by many a level mead,
And shadowing bluff that made the banks,
We glided winding under ranks
Of iris, and the golden reed;

And still as vaster grew the shore
And roll'd the floods in grander space,
The maidens gather'd strength and grace
And presence, lordlier than before;

And I myself, who sat apart
And watch'd them, wax'd in every limb;
I felt the thews of Anakim,
The pulses of a Titan's heart;

As one would sing the death of war,
And one would chant the history
Of that great race, which is to be,
And one the shaping of a star;

Until the forward-creeping tides
Began to foam, and we to draw
From deep to deep, to where we saw
A great ship lift her shining sides.

The man we loved was there on deck,
But thrice as large as man he bent
To greet us. Up the side I went,
And fell in silence on his neck;

Whereat those maidens with one mind
Bewail'd their lot; I did them wrong:
'We served thee here,' they said, 'so long,
And wilt thou leave us now behind?'

So rapt I was, they could not win
An answer from my lips, but he
Replying, 'Enter likewise ye
And go with us:' they enter'd in.

And while the wind began to sweep
A music out of sheet and shroud,
We steer'd her toward a crimson cloud
That landlike slept along the deep.

There is so much in this dream sequence that a grieving person might recognise: the perception of the belovèd as present but somehow veiled; our memories creating an image, a statue, like the person we love, but only a representation, not the real person we long for. And then the realisation that just as the friend who has died has made their own journey beyond the 'bourne of Time and Place', in Tennyson's words from his poem 'Crossing the Bar', so we too must make ours. It is as though the little departure, the business of moving house, somehow releases in Tennyson's dream-life an emblem or allegory of the greater leaving that lies ahead of him. But this emblematic dream of our last journey towards the heart of heaven suggests that even though outwardly our leaving seems a loss and a diminishment, that final voyage is a journey in which we will grow more deeply into the person we really are. So he writes:

> And still as vaster grew the shore
> And roll'd the floods in grander space,
> The maidens gather'd strength and grace
> And presence, lordlier than before;
>
> And I myself, who sat apart
> And watch'd them, wax'd in every limb

When Tennyson was asked who the maidens were in the dream, who dwelt with him in the hall and on the hidden summits, he answered, 'They are the Muses, poetry, arts – all that made life beautiful here, which we hope will pass with us beyond the grave.'

So as Tennyson's own summons comes he avails himself, not for the last time, of that primal symbol of the river as the stream of time and the sea as the eternity from which time comes and into which it flows. But this whole scene with the harp and the maidens, the 'little shallop' waiting, and beyond it the shining ship, is redolent of a poem he had already written in *Idylls of the King* about the death of King Arthur. In Tennyson's mind, that poem had become not only about the mythical Arthur but also about the man he loved. In the legend, Arthur's loyal knight Sir Bedivere brings the wounded king to the dusky barge where three veiled queens are mourning. Arthur tells him that the ship would take him

> To the island-valley of Avilion;
> Where falls not hail, or rain, or any snow,
> Nor ever wind blows loudly; but it lies
> Deep-meadowed, happy, fair with orchard lawns
> And bowery hollows crowned with summer sea,
> Where I will heal me of my grievous wound.

So now in *In Memoriam* Tennyson dreams that he is called to the same journey, and even before they reach that further shore he has a joyful reunion with the Arthur he loved. In a beautiful touch he sees how that love and grief are themselves the friends of the Muses who helped the poet give them voice. As Arthur tells the Muses, 'Enter likewise ye and go with us', we have the hope that in the resurrection nothing will be lost; all good gifts, even those that delighted us in this world, will find their place in heaven.

I sometimes wonder whether this poignant vision of Tennyson's is not one of the sources for the beautiful passage of the 'Grey Havens' at the very end of *The Lord of the Rings*. Frodo and Bilbo are taken up onto the shining ship that slips away down the long grey firth, and Tolkien tells us that the ship went out into the high sea and passed into the West. In the end, Frodo 'beheld white shores and beyond them a far green country under a swift sunrise', and it is to that swift sunrise, to the light of Easter Dawn, that we turn in the final part of this book.

36

Easter Dawn

Malcolm Guite

He blesses every love that weeps and grieves
And now he blesses hers who stood and wept
And would not be consoled, or leave her love's
Last touching place, but watched as low light crept
Up from the east. A sound behind her stirs
A scatter of bright birdsong through the air.
She turns, but cannot focus through her tears,
Or recognise the Gardener standing there.
She hardly hears his gentle question 'Why,
Why are you weeping?', or sees the play of light
That brightens as she chokes out her reply
'They took my love away, my day is night'
And then she hears her name, she hears Love say
The Word that turns her night, and ours, to Day.

This is the final poem in the sequence of 15 sonnets on the
Stations of the Cross which I published in *Sounding the Seasons*.
I originally intended there to be 14 sonnets, for the last station is
usually the fourteenth: 'Jesus is laid in the tomb'. My fourteenth
sonnet had finished with the lines:

He blesses every love that weeps and grieves
And makes our grief the pangs of a new birth.
The love that's poured in silence at old graves

Renewing flowers, tending the bare earth,
Is never lost. In him all love is found
And sown with him, a seed in the rich ground.

Before they were published, though, I shared the sequence of 14
with some friends, and one of those friends, whose husband had
recently died, wrote to me and said, 'Don't leave us here, this will
be my first Easter without my husband.' And she told me that
sometimes there is a 'fifteenth station' for the resurrection, and
would I write a fifteenth sonnet, that she might have an Easter
hope in that first season of grief? And so I wrote this final sonnet,
meditating on the great resurrection story in John 20.1–18 and
especially the encounter in verses 11–16:

> But Mary stood weeping outside the tomb. As she wept, she
> bent over to look into the tomb; and she saw two angels in
> white, sitting where the body of Jesus had been lying, one at the
> head and the other at the feet. They said to her, 'Woman, why
> are you weeping?' She said to them, 'They have taken away
> my Lord, and I do not know where they have laid him.' When
> she had said this, she turned round and saw Jesus standing
> there, but she did not know that it was Jesus. Jesus said to her,
> 'Woman, why are you weeping? For whom are you looking?'
> Supposing him to be the gardener, she said to him, 'Sir, if you
> have carried him away, tell me where you have laid him, and I
> will take him away.' Jesus said to her, 'Mary!' She turned and
> said to him in Hebrew, 'Rabbouni!' (which means Teacher).

That scene in the pre-dawn darkness of the garden of resur-
rection is perhaps the most moving in the Gospel. What comes
across is Mary Magdalene's tenacity in grief. The other disciples
have come and gone, but she stays where she is, still weeping.

Some years before I wrote this sonnet I was deeply moved by
these words in an Easter sermon by Lancelot Andrewes:

> But Marie went not, she stood still. Their going away com-
> mends her staying behinde. To the grave she came before them,

From the grave she stayes behind them. *Fortior eam figebat affectus*, saith Augustine, 'a stronger affection fixed her, so fixed her', that she had not the power to remove thence. Goe, who would, she would not, but stay, still. To stay while others doe so, while company stayes, that is the worlds love: But Peter is gone, and John too: all are gone, and we left alone; then to stay, is love, and constant love. *Amore manens, aliis recedentibus*, 'Love, that when others shrinke and give over, holds out still.'

The third in these, 'she stood, and she wept;' And, not a teare or two: but she wept a good (as we say;) That the Angels, That Christ himselfe pite her, and both of them, the first thing they doe, they aske her, Why wept she so? Both of them begin with that question. And, in this, is love.*

Love is at the heart of John's Gospel: Christ's love for us and ours for one another and for him. The 'good news' of the Easter Gospel is that the Divine Love cannot be killed and in the life of that Divine Love all our own loves, when they are given over to him, can also rise and live. This is not a vague and generalised hope, this is personal and particular resurrection; Mary's hope does not revive until she hears her own name, spoken in the familiar voice of the belovèd. God in Christ spoke us into being, and in Christ he will speak us into being again.

---

* Extract from a Sermon by Lancelot Andrewes on John 20.11–17, preached before King James I at Whitehall on Easter Day, 16 April 1620.

37

A Churchyard Song of Patient Hope

Christina Rossetti

All tears done away with the bitter unquiet sea,
Death done away from among the living at last,
Man shall say of sorrow – Love grant it to thee and me! –
At last, 'It is past.'

Shall I say of pain, 'It is past,' nor say it with thee,
Thou heart of my heart, thou soul of my soul, my Friend?
Shalt thou say of pain, 'It is past,' nor say it with me
Beloved to the end?

This short lyric is an intensely personal meditation on the famous
verses from Revelation (21.1–4), in which are concentrated so
many Christian hopes:

Then I saw a new heaven and a new earth; for the first heaven
and the first earth had passed away, and the sea was no more.
And I saw the holy city, the new Jerusalem, coming down out
of heaven from God, prepared as a bride adorned for her hus-
band. And I heard a loud voice from the throne saying, 'See,
the home of God is among mortals. He will dwell with them;
they will be his peoples, and God himself will be with them;
he will wipe every tear from their eyes. Death will be no more;
mourning and crying and pain will be no more, for the first
things have passed away.'

We can see how this poem responds to the scripture by combining and recombining elements of it in a new and living way. The passage from Revelation speaks of the sea being no more, also that there will be no more crying. Rossetti combines these two ideas in the opening line of her poem. It is as though she has gathered all the tears of the long, shadowed history of the world, the *rerum lacrimae*, as Virgil says, and poured them together into one 'bitter unquiet sea' which is to be no more. Death will be done away with at last. But rather than simply looking forward to that day, as a conventional poet might have done, Rossetti gives us a far more vivid and hopeful perspective: she invites us to imagine that it has already come and we are looking back on it together, united again with the friends we have lost, and saying together, 'It is past.'

But we almost miss what she is doing here. It is hard to construe the last lines of that first verse because in the midst of the sentence, 'Man shall say of sorrow … at last, "It is past"', she urgently interjects her own personal plea: 'Love grant it to thee and me!' She knows there will be a general resurrection but she is impatient to make it personal and so, in the next verse the voice of the poem changes to the first person. Rossetti is speaking in the churchyard to the one she has lost but is looking forward to the day when they can say together that their pain is over:

Shall I say of pain, 'It is past,' nor say it with thee,
Thou heart of my heart, thou soul of my soul, my Friend?

It can be very helpful to try to think of a day when we will have climbed out of that shadow and can look back on it even now, even while we are still in the 'valley of the shadow of death'. This poem of Rossetti's always puts me in mind of a much more recent lyric in the song 'Looking Forward' by the American band Over the Rhine:

Prayed last night
Dear God please no
But I was never good at letting go

I'm lookin' forward to lookin' back
On this day

None of us, in truth, are ever good at letting go. While this
anthology can be taken as a journey of 40 days, we will all pass
through its different staging posts many times and in different
orders in our grief. But at any moment our imagination can be
kindled through the gifts of poetry and song and shown at least
the possibility of looking forward to looking back. Although the
final word is 'end', the poem is not really about ending but about
beginning, beginning in 'a new heaven and a new earth' when
'Death will be no more; mourning and crying and pain will be no
more, for the first things have passed away.'

38

Death be Not Proud

John Donne

Death, be not proud, though some have called thee
Mighty and dreadful, for thou art not so;
For those whom thou think'st thou dost overthrow
Die not, poor Death, nor yet canst thou kill me.
From rest and sleep, which but thy pictures be,
Much pleasure; then from thee much more must flow,
And soonest our best men with thee do go,
Rest of their bones, and soul's delivery.
Thou art slave to fate, chance, kings, and desperate men,
And dost with poison, war, and sickness dwell,
And poppy or charms can make us sleep as well
And better than thy stroke; why swell'st thou then?
One short sleep past, we wake eternally
And death shall be no more; Death, thou shalt die.

In some ways this sonnet by a Dean of St Paul's Cathedral might seem to take us back to that sermon by a later Canon of St Paul's, Henry Scott Holland, which we discussed in the Introduction to this anthology. Donne, I think, has the better of his successor here, it is not that Death has always been 'nothing at all', but that death has been *made nothing*, because it has been *defeated*.

The first, contemporary readers of Donne's sonnet would have been familiar with the figure of Death carved on monuments and represented in paintings: the grim reaper, the skeletal

figure brandishing a scythe and lording it over fallen human-
ity with a pale crown on his head. Donne fully understood the
force of this image and his is not a poem of evasion but of con-
fident Christian courage rooted in the resurrection of Christ. So
the opening lines rebuke Death for pride, a wonderful satiric
reversal of the preachers' cliché that it is Death who rebukes
human pride. In the phrase 'though some have called thee mighty
and dreadful' Donne nods in the direction of those apocalyptic
pictures of Death triumphant, but then in words of one syllable
he cuts Death down to size, 'for thou art not so'. By the time we
reach the fourth line, Death is so reduced that we are invited
to have pity on him in his distress; 'poor Death'. Then in line 5
he opens up the archetypal analogy between sleep and death to
which he will return triumphantly in the final couplet. His argu-
ment in these lines is that if rest and sleep, which are like pictures
of death, give us both pleasure and refreshment, then even better
things may come from death itself. The last two lines of the octet
turn again on a common trope that it seems the best people die
young:

> And soonest our best men with thee do go,
> Rest of their bones, and soul's delivery.

In that last phrase, 'soul's delivery', Donne may be summoning
an image of new birth and perhaps consciously recalling lines by
an earlier poet, Sir John Davies, in which death is directly com-
pared with birth:

> Then doth th'aspiring Soul the body leave,
> Which we call Death; but were it known to all,
> What life our souls do by this death receive,
> Men would it birth or gaol delivery call.

Then at the start of the sestet Donne pours scorn and contumely
on death in the famous line 'Thou art slave to fate, chance, kings,
and desperate men', a grim comment on the fact that men summon
death as often as death summons them. All this is brought to a

head in the question at the end of line 12, 'why swell'st thou then?': why are you so proud and puffed up? The whole tone then changes in the final couplet which reaches out to include the reader: 'One short sleep past, we wake eternally'. Here we are once more in the great dawn of the resurrection garden. We hear that call of Christ, which Paul gives us in Ephesians 5.14:

> Sleeper, awake!
> Rise from the dead,
> and Christ will shine on you.

There is a wonderful contrast between the shortness and singleness of the sleep of death and the eternity of the great awakening beyond that sleep. The final line, 'And death shall be no more; Death, thou shalt die', brings the poem to a climax with a direct reference to the two verses from 1 Corinthians, 15.26 and 15.54, which have throughout been the real subject of the poem:

> The last enemy to be destroyed is death ... When this perishable body puts on imperishability, and this mortal body puts on immortality, then the saying that is written will be fulfilled: 'Death has been swallowed up in victory.'

39

Let Beauty Awake

Robert Louis Stevenson (stanzas 1–2),
Steve Bell (stanzas 3–4), N. T. Wright
(stanza 5)

Let Beauty awake in the morn from
beautiful dreams
Let Beauty awake from rest
Let Beauty awake
For Beauty's sake
In the hour when the birds awake in the brake
And the stars are yet bright in the west
Let Beauty awake from rest

Let Beauty awake in the eve from the
slumber of day
Awake in the crimson eve
In the day's dusk end
When the shades ascend
Let here wake to the kiss of a tender friend
To render again and receive
Let Beauty awake in the eve

While we, the gardeners of creation blessed
Furrow the soil at our Saviour's behest
And bury the seeds of our own life's death
And suffer God's glory to grow

Yes we, the priests of all that is made
Gather the greatness of creation's praise
That burgeoning freshness of glory displayed
From depths of the earth below

Let Beauty awake in the morn
From the cool of the grave
Beauty awake from death
Let Beauty awake
For Jesus' sake
In the hour when the angels their silence break
And the garden is bright with his breath
Let Beauty awake from death

Today's poem is the lyric of a song sung by the Canadian musician Steve Bell, and taken from his wonderful album *Where the Good Way Lies*. More than that, it is a collaboration across the continents and the centuries between the arts and the scriptures. For that reason it is also an epitome of what I hope to do in this anthology, bringing many disparate sources together in a single work, whose purpose is both to express grief and to renew hope.

The first two verses of this piece are themselves a complete poem by Robert Louis Stevenson and may be read in their own right. Bell, having decided to set this Stevenson poem to music, remembered that he had heard a third verse somewhere which he had particularly loved. Eventually, he tracked it down as being by the great New Testament scholar N. T. Wright, in a sermon on John 20.1–18, on that dawn in the garden of resurrection, preached when Wright was Bishop of Durham. Bell asked Wright if perhaps he had access to some fuller version of the Stevenson poem not published in anthologies, but it turned out that Wright had himself composed this final verse to draw the beauty of Stevenson's high romanticism into the deeper and more rooted beauty of the gospel. Working with this material from the nineteenth and twenty-first centuries, Bell realised that a middle section or 'bridge' was required to link the verses to make a song, and therefore wrote two further verses himself, which he inserted between Stevenson's lyric and Wright's coda. And from these three different strands of writing a new poem, a new 'whole' with its own form and beauty has emerged.

Preaching on Easter Day in Durham Cathedral, Wright had opened his sermon by reciting the first verse of the Stevenson poem, and then commented:

> Impossibly romantic, you will think. How could the Bishop allow Easter morning to be subverted, trivialized even, by Robert Louis Stevenson's high Victorian sentiment? Yes, all right, morning is indeed beautiful, and so for that matter is evening, as in the poem's second stanza; but how can you go back to that old romantic vision? Hasn't the whole twentieth century, not to mention what's already gone of the twenty-first, made it impossible to return to that dreamy, pre-Raphaelite world? Don't we have to be a lot tougher than that these days?

Wright went on to make the case for beauty both as part of the gospel and something that is desperately needed in the modern world.

> Among the many crises we face in our world is a crisis of beauty, and the fact that we can talk at length about everything else – money, the environment, sex, political corruption, not to mention Newcastle United – and only bring in beauty as an afterthought tells its own story. Perhaps it's time to turn things round the other way, and start with the question of beauty and work in from there.

After a beautiful exposition of the Gospel itself, Wright asks:

> But what has it got to do with beauty?
> Everything. Perhaps surprisingly, the word 'beauty' occurs very seldom in the Bible. When it does, there are two main focal points; human beauty (often with a health warning; this doesn't last!) and, particularly, the beauty of the Temple. If this

is the place where the living God is to dwell, against the day when he will flood the whole of his beautiful creation with his presence, then the Temple must be made, and was made, as a supreme object of beauty.

Yes, it is true that beauty divorced from goodness and truth, cut off from its origin in the beauty of God, may decay into a mere indulgent aestheticism, but the resurrection of Jesus in that beautiful garden gives a chance to begin again, rooting beauty where it really belongs.

After all, if new creation has begun, if beauty has awoken afresh in the new Temple, the living home of the living God, as he awakens from the tomb, and if beauty is now let loose in all the world, it will rightly generate new forms, new possibilities, new delights. It will come closer and closer to its two senior cousins, Love and Truth, showing with them how to avoid the other false polarization, a brittle objectivity and a collapsing subjectivity, because it will be kept in place by the work of image-bearing, Spirit-filled human beings as they reflect the glory of God into the world and the glory of the world back to God.

It is at that moment in the sermon that Wright gives his own verse:

Let Beauty awake, in the morn
From the cool of the grave
Beauty awake from death;
Let Beauty awake,
For Jesus' sake,
In the hour when the angels their silence break
And the garden is bright with his Breath.
Let Beauty awake from death

Bell's verses deepen the theme even further. We are not simply the detached beholders of God's aesthetic, looking in on beauty's garden from the outside. We too are called to be gardeners along with Christ, to

Furrow the soil at our Saviour's behest
And bury the seeds of our own life's death
And suffer God's glory to grow

There is a wonderful double sense in Bell's use of the word 'suffer' here. In the older sense it means to allow something to happen, but of course it must carry the modern sense too. Somehow, our own suffering offered to God might become not only a furrowing of the soil but the sowing of the seed; every little act of letting go can be a sowing of 'the seed of our own life's death'; those who sow in tears will reap with songs of joy. But Bell does not use the 'sow', he uses the word 'bury', and surely that is to give some gospel, some good news, to those who mourn, those who feel in their grief that they have buried their life's best hopes.

In the second of his stanzas, Bell moves us on from being gardeners to being 'the priests of all that is made' who 'gather the greatness of creation's praise ... from the depths of the earth below'. Here there may be a gentle allusion to the work of two other poets. In his poem 'Providence' George Herbert says:

Man is the worlds high Priest: he doth present
The sacrifice for all; while they below
Unto the service mutter an assent,
Such as springs use that fall, and winds that blow.

And in 'God's Grandeur', Gerard Manley Hopkins speaks of how the grandeur and glory of God, charged into the very being of the world, will 'gather to a greatness'. Bell fuses these two sources and calls us, even in the midst of our grief, to be the priests who help to gather that greatness. What gives us the courage to do so, what wakens us to the greatness of our calling? It is the good news that beauty itself has awoken in Christ 'From the cool of the grave'; 'the garden is bright with his breath' as Beauty awakes 'from death'.

40

Crossing the Bar

Alfred, Lord Tennyson

Sunset and evening star,
And one clear call for me!
And may there be no moaning of the bar,
When I put out to sea,

But such a tide as moving seems asleep,
Too full for sound and foam,
When that which drew from out the boundless deep
Turns again home.

Twilight and evening bell,
And after that the dark!
And may there be no sadness of farewell,
When I embark;

For tho' from out our bourne of Time and Place
The flood may bear me far,
I hope to see my Pilot face to face
When I have crost the bar.

In the introduction to each part of this book we have been guided by Tennyson, and it seems good in this final poem to bring him back into the main text. This perfect little lyric was written on board a ship in 1889, towards the end of his life, while he was crossing the Solent between the mainland and his home on the Isle of Wight. The poem apparently came to Tennyson spontaneously and he immediately ducked into his cabin and jotted it down. That evening he read it to his friend W. F. Rawnsley, who tells us: 'When he repeated it to me in the evening, I said "that is the crown of your life's work." He answered, "It came in a moment."'

The poem was published that year, and Tennyson added a note to his editor, which all his subsequent editors have respected: 'Mind you put my "Crossing the Bar" at the end of all editions of my poems.' Like the passage from *In Memoriam* we used in the introduction to this last part of this anthology, this poem seems to touch on Tennyson's visionary lines in 'Morte d'Arthur' about the great King Arthur being taken on board the mysterious ship and setting out for Avalon. In the final recension of that poem, Tennyson said of the passing of Arthur: 'from the great deep to the great deep he goes'.

The 'bar' in this poem is a reference to the often dangerous sand or shingle bank that lies across a harbour mouth. These harbour bars shift and vary in depth and position and can give rise to short, tumbled seas. It often requires the knowledge of an expert local pilot to guide the ship through. You might be able to leave your local harbour without the help of pilot, sailing clear over the bar, perhaps on a rising tide, but to cross the bar of a new and unknown harbour you would need a pilot. This poem gently enacts that journey. In that first verse at twilight, beneath the evening star, Tennyson and the reader are putting out to sea, crossing over the harbour bar of this familiar life, moved by a tide that is turning as it must. The tide that poured into the harbour of our earthly life is now withdrawing as we come to twilight and the evening of our days.

The second verse is, in one sense, simply referring to the tide itself: 'such a tide as moving seems asleep', a tide 'which drew from out the boundless deep', turning again home. But on another level 'that which drew from out the boundless deep' is not just the tide but the soul itself, turning again home. In the third verse, the parting soul embarks, sailing out towards the sunset and beyond it. For from the perspective of those who stand on the shore and watch us going, we are sailing out into the dark. But these are not the final words. In the fourth stanza, it is as though the dying person himself turns to give comfort to the bereaved, to share with them the hope he already has:

> For tho' from out our bourne of Time and Place
> The flood may bear me far,
> I hope to see my Pilot face to face
> When I have crost the bar.

This is clear and simple language and yet it is rich with a powerful gathering and echo of other great texts. Perhaps that phrase 'from out our bourne of Time and Place' is a reply to Hamlet's comment on death as 'the undiscovered country from whose bourn no traveller returns' (*Hamlet*, Act III, Scene I). On the contrary, says Tennyson, this world of time and place is the shadowed bourn and we sail through death to a better country. Of course, the whole notion of going through the dark towards an encounter where we will at last be face to face with God is drawing richly on 1 Corinthians 13.12: 'For now we see in a mirror, dimly, but then we will see face to face. Now I know only in part; then I will know fully, even as I have been fully known.'

The final image of Christ as the Pilot is wonderful. In order to help any ship cross the bar, the pilot must have entered the harbour himself, must have already pioneered the passage and know how to cross the bar. So it is with Christ, who goes ahead of us through death, secures the path and opens up the way, as the psalmist prophetically intuited in Psalm 23.4:

> Even though I walk through the darkest valley,
> I fear no evil;
> for you are with me;
> your rod and your staff –
> they comfort me.

Tennyson himself once commented on these lines, 'the pilot has been on board all the while, but in the dark I have not seen him'. So this poem, too, is in the end about our passage through the night, our arrival at that Easter dawn and awakening, when at last we see, face to face, the One who has journeyed with us through our grief, the only One who can speak the word to us that turns our night to day.

References

Bell, Steve, 'Let Beauty Awake', music by Steve Bell, stanzas by Robert Louis Stevenson, Steve Bell and N. T. Wright. From the album *Where the Good Way Lies*, Signpost Music Limited, 2016.

Belloc, Hilaire, 'I Went to Sleep at Dawn in Tuscany', 'Mortality is but the Stuff you wear', *Complete Verse*, ed. A. N. Wilson, Pimlico, 1991.

Belmonte, Kelly, 'Misunderstood in Late 20th Century Scotland', previously unpublished.

Browning, Elizabeth Barrett, 'Grief', first published in E. B. Barrett, *Poems*, Edward Moxon, London, 1844.

Cairns, Scott, 'Threnody', 'Another Kiss', *Slow Pilgrim: The Collected Poems*, Paraclete Press, 2015.

Donne, John, 'Death be Not Proud' (1609), *Songs and Sonnets*, published posthumously in 1633.

Duffy, Carol Ann, 'Prayer', *Mean Time*, Anvil Press, 1994.

Faber, Michel, 'Lucencies' and 'Lucencies (2)', *Undying: A Love Story*, Canongate Books, 2016.

Guite, Malcolm, 'Earth', 'Holding and Letting Go', *The Singing Bowl*, Canterbury Press, 2013.

Guite, Malcolm, 'Easter Dawn', *Sounding the Seasons*, Canterbury Press, 2012.

Guite, Malcolm, 'Let Not Your Hearts Be Troubled', *Parable and Paradox*, Canterbury Press, 2015.

Guite, Malcolm, 'Remembrance Sunday Afternoon', previously unpublished.

Hardy, Thomas, 'The Going', 'The Voice', *Satires of Circumstance: Lyrics and Reveries*, Macmillan, 1914.

Herbert, George, 'Bitter-Sweet', *The Temple*, 1633.

Holland, Henry Scott, 'Death is Nothing at All', extract from a sermon preached in St Paul's Cathedral, London, Sunday 15 May 1910, just after the death of Edward VII.

Jonson, Ben, 'On My First Son', included in First Folio, 1616.

Lindop, Grevel, 'Scattering the Ashes', *Playing With Fire*, Carcanet Press, 2006.

Ordway, Holly, 'Paradigm Shift: Angelus', 'A Sudden Goldfinch', *Apologetics and the Christian Imagination: An Integrated Approach to Defending the Faith*, Emmaus Road, 2017.

Ó Tuama, Pádraig, 'All Around', published with the permission of the poet.

Over the Rhine, 'Looking Forward', *Drunkard's Prayer*, Back Porch Records, 2005.

Rice, Adrian, 'The Grieving Ground', 'The Double Crown', *The Clock Flower*, Moongate Publications, 2012.

Rossetti, Christina, 'A Churchyard Song of Patient Hope', *Verses*, SPCK, 1894.

Scott, David, 'Flower Rota', *Playing for England*, Bloodaxe Books, 1989.

Shakespeare, William, *Hamlet* (1600).

Shakespeare, William, *King John* (1596).

Shaw, Luci, 'Onlookers', *Polishing the Petoskey Stone*, Shaw Publishers, 1990.

Shaw, Luci, 'Our Prayers Break on God', 'To What End this First and Final Life', previously unpublished.

Shelley, Percy Bysshe, *Adonais* (1821).

Tennyson, Alfred Lord, 'Crossing the Bar', *Demeter and Other Poems*, Macmillan and Co., 1889.

Tennyson, Alfred Lord, *In Memoriam*, Edward Moxon, London, 1850.

Vaughan, Henry, 'They are all gone into the world of light' (1653), *Silex Scintillans*, 1655.

Ward, Frances, 'Harbouring Christ', previously unpublished.

Ward, Michael, 'Rest Lake', previously unpublished.

Wordsworth, William, 'Surprised by Joy' (1815).

Worskett, Nicholas, 'Their Parting', previously unpublished.

Wright, N. T., extracts from 'Let Beauty Awake', sermon preached in Durham Cathedral on Easter Day 2009, www.ntwrightpage.com.

Acknowledgements

I am grateful to my editor Christine Smith for suggesting I make this anthology and also for suggesting its evocative title. I am also indebted to a number of poets who appear in this volume for permission to use their work. Steve Bell, Kelly Belmonte, Scott Cairns, Michel Faber, Holly Ordway, Pádraig Ó Tuama, Luci Shaw, Frances Ward, Michael Ward, and N. T. Wright all granted personal permission, as well as permission from their publishers, and many of them have provided helpful conversations and correspondence about their poems as I worked on this anthology. I am in addition grateful for the following specific publishing permissions:

'Prayer' from *Mean Time* by Carol Ann Duffy. Published by Anvil Press Poetry, 1993. Copyright © Carol Ann Duffy. Reproduced by permission of the author c/o Rogers, Coleridge & White Ltd, 20 Powis Mews, London W11 1JN.

'The Grieving Ground' and 'The Double Crown' by Adrian Rice, from *The Clock Flower* (Press 53, 2013).

'Flower Rota' by David Scott from *Beyond the Drift: New & Selected Poems* (Bloodaxe Books, 2015). Reproduced with permission of Bloodaxe Books. www.bloodaxebooks.com.

'Let Beauty Awake' by N. T. Wright. Reproduced by permission of the author.

'Scattering the Ashes' by Grevel Lindop from *Playing With Fire* (Carcanet Press Limited 2006). Reproduced with permission of Carcanet Press Limited.

'Lucencies' and 'Lucencies (2)' by Michel Faber from *Undying* (Canongate Books 2016). Reproduced by kind permission of Canongate Books.

'Looking Forward', by Linford Detweiler and Karin Bergquist of Over the Rhine, on the album *Drunkard's Prayer* (Back Porch Records, 2005).

ACKNOWLEDGEMENTS

I would never have completed this book without the love and understanding of my family, and the immense practical help from Judith Tonry who acted as my amanuensis throughout, and from Philippa Pearson who assisted me in many administrative and permissions tasks.

Finally, I am grateful to the many friends, parishioners, colleagues and students who have, over the years, shared their grief with me and trusted me to take the funerals of those they loved. If there is any wisdom in this book it comes from them.

CPSIA information can be obtained
at www.ICGtesting.com
Printed in the USA
LVOW11s0043280418
575140LV00002BA/200/P